AF316701

CUSTOMER SERVICE SKILLS

UNDERSTAND YOUR CUSTOMERS & SERVE THEM EFFECTIVELY

BY

MULUALEM HAGOS

CUSTOMER SERVICE SKILLS

TABLE OF CONTENTS

ABOUT THE AUTHOR

Mulualem Hagos is a devoted husband, father, and leader, known for his unwavering commitment to spreading hope and transforming lives. He is married to Ruth Hagos, and together they are proud parents of three children: Philip, Sophia, and Caleb. Family is at the heart of Mulualem's life, providing him with inspiration and motivation to pursue his mission of service and support.

MINISTRY AND MISSION WORK

For Mulualem, God is the foundation of everything. He has dedicated his life to serving God and fulfilling His will by spreading the Gospel. As the founder and president of the Good Samaritan Prison Ministry and Mulualem Hagos Ministry, Mulualem has committed himself to helping those who are incarcerated and feel lost. Guided by the mission motto, "Changing lives one person at a time," his work emphasizes hope, compassion, and rehabilitation for individuals in prison. Under his leadership, the ministry has successfully planted churches in several countries, offering spiritual guidance and practical support to inmates in local prisons.

Through his tireless efforts, Mulualem has profoundly impacted countless lives, offering more than just spiritual guidance but also practical support to those in need. His ministry has become a beacon of hope for many, illustrating the transformative power of faith and community.

PROFESSIONAL JOURNEY

In addition to his ministry, Mulualem is a multifaceted professional. He serves as a pastor at a local church and has an entrepreneurial spirit that has led him to explore various business ventures. These ventures allow him to combine his passion for service with innovative solutions to community challenges.

As an author, Mulualem shares his insights and experiences in books that inspire others. He is also a life coach and counselor, using his expertise to guide individuals through their personal journeys. As a public speaker, he addresses diverse audiences, sharing messages of hope, resilience, and the importance of community support.

VALUES AND VISION

Mulualem Hagos stands firm in his belief that every individual has the potential for change and growth. His work reflects a deep commitment to empowering others, fostering hope, and promoting healing within communities. With empathy and compassion, he approaches each challenge with the desire to uplift those around him.

Through his ministry, professional work, and community leadership, Mulualem continues to inspire and lead by example. His unwavering faith and dedication show that with support, determination, and a shared sense of purpose, lives can be transformed for the better.

DEDICATION

This book is dedicated to Yosef Asgedom,

Yosef Asgedom was born and raised in the vibrant city of Addis Ababa, Ethiopia. የቄር ልኞ. From a young age, he exhibited a keen interest in entrepreneurship, driven by a desire to create and innovate. Growing up in a city rich with culture and creativity, Yosef was inspired by his father, Asgodom Woldemichel, and his loving mother, ማጣ ግዳዬ. His journey would not only lead him to success but also empower countless others along the way.

Yosef is the founder and CEO of Liwa Trading PLC, which manages various import and export businesses.

With determination and a visionary mindset, Yosef founded a successful printing company that rapidly gained traction in both Ethiopia and Uganda. His venture became known for its quality and reliability, servinga diverse client base while fostering growth in the local economy. Under his leadership, the company thrived for years, a testament to his business acumen and dedication.

Beyond his entrepreneurial pursuits, Yosef is passionate about mentorship and helping young aspirants realize their dreams. He has taken on the role of a guide, sharing his experiences and expertise with aspiring entrepreneurs, providing them with the tools and confidence they need to succeed. His commitment to fostering the next generation of business leaders has been a driving force in his life.

In addition to mentoring, Yosef has engaged in counseling, offering support and guidance to those navigating their personal and professional journeys. His empathy and understanding have made a profound impact on many, inspiring them to overcome obstacles and chase their ambitions.

Yosef Asgedom's journey is not just one of personal success; it is a legacy of inspiration, empowerment, and community upliftment. Through his work, he continues to shape the future of entrepreneurship in Ethiopia and beyond, proving that with passion, determination, and a willingness to help others, one can create a lasting impact on the world.

CHAPTER 1:
INTRODUCTION - THE
ART OF SERVING OTHERS

In the quiet town of Willow Creek, nestled between rolling hills and meandering rivers, there stood a little bakery that seemed to defy all logic. The bakery was modest, with a faded sign swinging on rusted chains and a storefront that hadn't been updated in decades. The wooden door creaked every time a customer entered, and the mismatched chairs inside wobbled on uneven legs. Yet, despite its humble appearance, the bakery, known as Grace's Corner, was always full. From the crack of dawn until the sun dipped behind the hills, customers came in droves—locals, travelers, tourists, young families, and even the town's elderly residents, who shuffled in daily to buy their favorite treats.

Behind the counter stood Grace, a woman whose silver hair was always neatly tied back, and whose hands were forever dusted with flour. Grace wasn't just the owner of the bakery; she was its heart and soul. She had been running it for over forty years, and during that time, she had witnessed generations of customers walk through her doors. Babies had grown into adults, and those adults now brought their own children to taste the bread and pastries that had become legendary in the town.

But Grace's Corner wasn't famous because of the pastries. Sure, her bread was good—no, it was great. It was baked fresh every morning, using simple ingredients and an old family recipe that had been passed down through generations. Her pies were flaky and golden, her cakes moist and perfectly sweet, and her cookies had just the right amount of chewiness. But what kept people coming back, what made Grace's bakery stand out from the fancier establishments in town, was something much more profound than flour, butter, and sugar.

Grace had an extraordinary gift. She wasn't just a baker; she was a nurturer, a listener, and above all, a master of the art of serving others. Every customer who walked through her door felt like they were the most important person in the world. She knew their names, their stories, their joys, and their sorrows. She remembered their favorite orders and had them ready before they even asked. She listened to their problems, offered words of comfort, and celebrated their successes. In Grace's bakery, people didn't just buy bread; they found companionship, understanding, and a sense of belonging.

The magic of Grace's Corner wasn't something you could measure or quantify. It wasn't in the price of the goods, the speed of the service, or even the quality of the pastries. It was in the way people felt when they walked through the door. It was in the warmth of Grace's smile, the sound of her laughter, and the way she made every customer feel like they were part of something special. For Grace, the bakery was more than just a business. It was her way of serving others, and of giving back to the community that had supported her for so many years.

One day, a young man named Sam wandered into Willow Creek. Sam was an ambitious entrepreneur, fresh out of business school, and eager to make his mark on the world. He had studied the latest trends in business, read every book on entrepreneurship, and developed a sleek, modern business plan. His dream was to open a chain of coffee shops that would rival the biggest names in the industry. He had investors lined up, a brand identity ready to go, and a marketing strategy that was sure to bring in customers.

But Sam had a problem. Despite his extensive knowledge and all the right tools, he couldn't seem to figure out the secret to building a loyal customer base. Everywhere he went, he saw coffee shops, bakeries, and cafes struggling to keep customers. They would open with a bang, but after a few months, the excitement would fade, and soon, they were offering discounts just to get people in the door. Sam didn't want that for his business. He wanted something sustainable, something that would stand the test of time.

As Sam strolled through Willow Creek, he noticed the line outside Grace's bakery. It was a small town, but the bakery was buzzing with activity. People were standing in line, chatting, laughing, and patiently waiting for their turn. Curious, Sam joined the queue, wondering what all the fuss was about. When he finally reached the counter, Grace greeted him with a smile.

"Good morning, young man," she said warmly. "What can I get for you today?"

Sam glanced at the display case, filled with an array of baked goods that, while tempting, didn't seem particularly extraordinary. "What's your secret?" he asked, his business mind kicking into gear. "How do you keep this place so busy?"

Grace smiled again, her eyes crinkling at the corners. "My secret? Oh, there's no secret, really. I just take care of my customers. I listen to them, I care about them, and I make sure they leave here feeling better than when they came in."

Sam frowned. "But what about the product? Isn't it all about the quality ofthe food? The marketing? The pricing?"

Grace shook her head gently. "Those things matter, of course. But they're not what keeps people coming back. You see, Sam, people don't just come here for the bread. They come because they know they're welcome here. They come because they know I care about them. I remember their names,their stories, their favorite pastries. I listen when they have something on their minds, and I celebrate with them when they have good news. That's what makes the difference."

Sam was perplexed. He had always thought that business success was about numbers, strategy, and market research. But here was this elderlywoman, running a bakery that defied all the conventional wisdom he had been taught, and yet, she was thriving.

Over the next few days, Sam returned to Grace's Corner, watching and learning. He observed how Grace interacted with her customers, how she took the time to listen to them, and how she treated each one as if they were the most important person in the room. It wasn't just about the transaction for Grace—it was about the relationship. It was about making people feel valued, understood, and appreciated.

Sam realized that Grace had tapped into something profound, something that no business school had ever taught him: the art of serving others.

THE HEART OF SERVICE

In the business world, customer service is often seen as a department, arole, or a line item on the budget. It's something businesses provide because they have to, not because they want to. But for Grace, and for successful businesses like hers, customer service isn't just a function—it's the heart and soul of everything they do. It's the difference between a business that survives and one that thrives.

Grace understood that people don't just buy products—they buy experiences. They buy feelings. They buy relationships. When a customer walks into your business, they're not just looking for a loaf of bread, a cupof coffee, or a new pair of shoes. They're looking for something deeper— connection, understanding, and value.

This is why businesses that excel in customer service often outperformthose that don't, even if their products aren't the best or their prices aren't the lowest. People will return to a business where they feel cared for, even if it means spending a little more or going out of their way.

Grace had mastered this art. She knew that every interaction with a customer was an opportunity to build a relationship, to make someone's day a little brighter, and to create a lasting impression. It wasn't about the bread—it was about the connection.

THE RIPPLE EFFECT OF GOOD SERVICE

As Sam continued to watch Grace work her magic, he began

to understand the ripple effect of good service. When you treat customers with care and respect, they don't just come back—they bring others with them. Word of mouth is one of the most powerful forms of marketing, and it can't be bought or faked. It has to be earned, one interaction at a time.

Grace's bakery had never needed to advertise. She didn't have a website, social media presence, or flashy signs. Yet, her business flourished. People came from all over because they had heard about Grace's Corner from a friend, a family member, or a colleague. The experience was so memorable, so positive, that they couldn't help but tell others.

This ripple effect is something every business owner dreams of, but few achieve. It takes time, patience, and a genuine commitment to serving others. It requires putting the customer's needs first, even when it's inconvenient or costly. But the rewards are immense. When customers feel valued, they become loyal advocates for your business. They spread the word, they bring their friends, and they keep coming back.

THE LONG GAME

Grace wasn't interested in quick wins or short-term profits. She understood that building a successful business was a long game. It wasn't about making as much money as possible in the shortest amount of time—it was about creating something lasting, something that would stand the test of time.

In today's fast-paced, profit-driven world, this approach may seem outdated or unrealistic. But Grace knew that the businesses that survived were the ones that invested in relationships. They were the ones that took the time to understand their customers, to meet their needs, and to exceed their expectations. These businesses didn't rely on gimmicks or discounts to attract customers—they relied on the trust and loyalty they had builtover time.

Sam realized that this was the key to building his own business. It wasn't enough to have a great product or a sleek marketing plan. He needed to focus on the customer, to understand their needs, and to create an experience that would keep them coming back.

BUILDING YOUR LEGACY

As Sam stood at the edge of Willow Creek, ready to embark on the next chapter of his life, he found himself reflecting on all that had transpiredduring his time there. It was not a large town, and on the surface, it seemed like a quiet, unassuming place. But the lessons it imparted to him were profound. For the first time in his entrepreneurial journey, Sam felt a deep sense of clarity and purpose. He realized that the success of a business wasn't simply measured by its products, profit margins, or growth charts—it was rooted in something far deeper. It was about people. It was about serving others with integrity, building meaningful relationships, and striving to leave a lasting legacy that transcended material success.

Sam's thoughts drifted to Grace and her small, yet beloved bakery, a place that had become a cornerstone of the community. Grace's Corner wasn't just a business; it was an embodiment of her spirit, her heart, and her life's work. Every loaf of bread, every cake, every pastry she meticulously crafted, carried with it her dedication, her love, and her commitment toexcellence.

But beyond the recipes and the flour-dusted countertops, Grace's bakery was a living testament to the power of service. She didn't just sell baked goods; she nourished the souls of the people who walked through her door. For Grace, every customer was more than just a transaction—they were part of her extended family. Each warm smile she offered and each kind word she spoke had a ripple effect that touched people's lives in ways she might never fully know.

Sam recalled the first time he stepped into Grace's Corner. He had beendriven by the idea of success, thinking about how to make his mark, howto get ahead in a competitive world. Back then, he measured achievement by how much he could accumulate—clients, revenue, accolades. But watching Grace, day after day, he came to understand something essential. Success wasn't just about what you got; it was about what you gave. Grace's bakery stood as a symbol of that truth, a beacon of light in the lives of so many. Her unwavering belief in kindness, her passion for her work, and her commitment to her community had made her business thrive in ways that numbers alone could never explain.

As Sam prepared to leave Willow Creek, those lessons resonated deeply within him. He thought about the way Grace greeted each person who entered her bakery—not as a customer, but as a cherished guest. She knew many of their names, remembered their favorite treats, and took the time to ask how their day was going. For Grace, the relationships she cultivated were as important, if not more so, than the products she sold. She had builtsomething truly remarkable—a business that was not only financially successful but also deeply fulfilling on a human level. It was her legacy. And in that legacy, Sam found inspiration.

The bakery, with its warm, inviting atmosphere, had become a place where people could find solace, joy, and connection. Sam often noticed how patrons lingered after buying their bread or pastries, sipping coffee at one of the small, round tables by the window. It wasn't just the smell of freshly baked goods that kept them there—it was the feeling of being seen, valued, and cared for. Grace had created something that went beyond the physical space of her bakery; she had fostered a sense of belonging. People came not only to satisfy their hunger but to experience the warmth of community that Grace had so lovingly cultivated.

Sam knew that this was what he wanted for his own business—a space that didn't just meet the demands of the market but met the deeper needs of people. He envisioned his coffee shop as more than just a place to grab a cup of coffee. He wanted it to be a refuge for those seeking connection, a place where strangers could become friends, where regulars would be greeted by name, and where everyone who walked through the door would feel like they mattered.

The lessons he learned in Willow Creek were not the kind taught in business schools or written about in management books. They were the kind that could only be absorbed through lived experience, through the quiet observation of someone like Grace, who understood the true essence of service. He would always remember her—not just for the exceptional bakery she ran but for the way she made people feel. The warmth of her smile, the sound of her laughter, and the way she listened intently, as if each conversation was the most important one in the world, had left an indelible mark on his heart.

As Sam moved forward to open his first coffee shop, he

carried Grace's wisdom with him like a precious gift. He no longer saw himself as merely selling coffee; he saw himself as creating an experience, a moment of respite in the hurried lives of his customers. He wanted his shop to be a place where people felt understood, appreciated, and valued. Whether they came in for a quick cup of coffee before work or spent hours working on a project at one of the tables, Sam was committed to making every interaction count. He wanted to build a community within the four walls of his shop, a space where people could connect, share stories, and find comfort.

As the sun set on his time in Willow Creek, Sam realized that his journey was just beginning. The lessons he had learned from Grace would serve as the foundation for everything he built moving forward. And in time, he hoped that, like Grace, he too would create a legacy—not just of success in business but of service, kindness, and human connection. He knew that if he stayed true to those values, his coffee shop would be more than just a place to get a drink—it would become a cherished part of the community, just as Grace's bakery had been.

With a deep breath and a heart full of gratitude, Sam turned toward his new venture, ready to carry forward the spirit of Willow Creek into the next chapter of his life. The journey ahead was unknown, but one thing was certain: the lessons of Grace's Corner would stay with him forever.

CONCLUSION

In the end, the art of serving others is the foundation of any successful business. It's the key to building lasting relationships, creating loyal customers, and leaving a legacy that goes beyond profits and products. It's about understanding that every interaction with a customer is an opportunity to make a positive impact, to brighten someone's day, and to create a lasting impression.

So, whether you're just starting out in business or you've been in the game for years, remember Grace's bakery. Remember that it's not just aboutwhat you sell—it's about how you make people feel. It's about the art of serving others.

And that, more than anything else, is the secret to lasting success.

CHAPTER 2: WHAT IS CUSTOMERSERVICE?

Let's take a journey, one that ventures far beyond the common understanding of "customer service." Picture this: a small, unassuming bakery nestled in the heart of a charming town, where cobblestone streets wind through clusters of local shops. The bakery, "Ella's Oven," had earned its reputation not merely for its mouth-watering sourdough, but for something far more elusive yet vital to its success: the way it made people feel.

Ella, the bakery's founder, had worked tirelessly for years, perfecting not only her recipes but the entire experience of walking through the door. People came for more than the bread, though that was reason enough. They came because the moment they stepped inside; they felt an unmistakable warmth. Not just from the oven, but from Ella herself. She greeted eachcustomer by name, always with a smile that seemed to say, "I'm so glad you're here."

For instance, Mrs. Thompson, a widow who had been coming to Ella'sOven for over a decade, was always greeted with a special Apricot Danish, warm and ready. Ella remembered that it was Mrs. Thompson's favorite treat, something her late husband used to bring home every Friday afternoon. For Ella, remembering this detail wasn't a clever business strategy; it was an act of care. It was about paying attention, showing empathy, and recognizing that her customers weren't just patrons, but individuals with stories, lives, and emotions.

Then there was young Emily, a shy teenager who came in

every Saturday morning, ordering the same extra crusty sourdough loaf. Ella knew thatEmily loved the bread, but more than that, Ella knew that Emily came because, in a world that often overlooked her, Ella saw her. "Here's your bread, just the way you like it," Ella would say, handing the bag over with a gentle wink. Emily would smile, a little brighter each week, knowingthat for those few minutes, she mattered.

Ella's success didn't stem only from the quality of her baked goods; it came from the heart she poured into serving her customers. Her bakerybecame more than a shop—it became a sanctuary. For the early risers, the regulars, and the occasional passerby, Ella's Oven was a place where they felt seen, appreciated, and understood. It was a place where they weren't just another face in the crowd, but someone who mattered.

But as the years went by, the bakery expanded. Ella opened another location, hired more staff, and eventually, she wasn't able to personally greet every customer. The bread was still just as good, the décor still just as cozy, but slowly, something started to change.

The familiar faces that had once lined up every morning began to dwindle. The lines weren't as long, and the energy wasn't as warm. Ella's heart ached as she watched the shift happen, seemingly beyond her control. At first, she couldn't understand it—nothing about the recipes had changed. The bread was still baked with the same precision, the coffee brewed to the same perfection. So why, she wondered, did it feel like the magic was fading?

One quiet afternoon, Ella found herself reflecting on what had made herbakery so special in the first place. As she gazed out of the window at the nearly empty street, it dawned on her. It wasn't just the bread that had built her business; it was the experience. It was the warmth, the care, the small moments of connection that she had shared with each customer. And that, she realized, was what had been lost in the expansion. The soul of customer service had slipped away amid the hustle and growth.

WHAT IS CUSTOMER SERVICE, REALLY?

Customer service isn't just about fulfilling a need or providing a product. It's about human connection. It's about understanding that every transaction is an opportunity to build a relationship, to make someone feel valued and appreciated. But to truly grasp the depth of customer service, we must go beyond the surface-level tasks of smiling politely, answering questions, or apologizing for mistakes.

Customer service, in its purest form, is emotional labor. It requires the ability to understand and anticipate the feelings of others, to be present in the moment, and to create an experience that makes people feel not only satisfied but uplifted.

Let's shift the lens a bit. Imagine a young woman named Clara. Clara is about to embark on one of the most significant and emotionally charged journeys of her life—shopping for her wedding dress. She's excited but also nervous. She's already visited several bridal shops, each with beautiful gowns, yet something about the experience felt…off. The salespeople were kind enough, but their compliments felt rehearsed, their advice distant. Each interaction left Clara feeling like just another bride in a long line of customers.

Then, one afternoon, Clara finds herself at a small bridal

boutique tucked away on a quiet street. The moment she steps inside, the atmosphere feels different. A woman named Maria, the consultant, greets her, not with a sales pitch or a rushed, "How can I help you?" but with a warm smile and a genuine question: "Tell me about your wedding. What are you dreaming of?"

Maria doesn't just want to sell Clara a dress—she wants to understand Clara's vision, her emotions, her excitement. Maria listens, truly listens, as Clara describes the venue, the color scheme, the feeling she wants to evoke on her special day. As they talk, Clara realizes she's not just another bride in a sea of customers to Maria—she's Clara, a unique individual with her own dreams and anxieties.

When Maria finally pulls a dress for Clara to try on, it's not just a random gown—it's the gown. The one that matches everything Clara described, down to the smallest detail. And when Clara puts it on, something magical happens. She doesn't just see herself in a wedding dress; she sees herself on her wedding day, surrounded by love, walking down the aisle toward her future. It's a transformative moment, one that Clara will never forget. And it wasn't the dress that made it happen—it was Maria's care, attention, and understanding.

THE IMPORTANCE OF CONNECTION IN CUSTOMER SERVICE

But customer service isn't always about grand moments like finding the perfect wedding dress. Sometimes, it's about how you handle the small, everyday situations—especially when things go wrong. Let's consider James, a hardworking man who's had a long, exhausting day. On his way home, he stops by a fast-food restaurant, craving a quick, no-fuss meal. He orders, pays, and heads home, only to discover that his order is completely wrong. His frustration spikes—he's hungry, tired, and now he's dealing with a mistake that shouldn't have happened.

Many people would simply accept the situation, perhaps with a grumble or a negative review. But James decides to call the restaurant. When he dials, he expects to hear the typical, impersonal response: "We're sorry for the inconvenience. Please come back, and we'll fix it." But that's not what happens. Instead, he's greeted by Rebecca, the manager on duty, who listens carefully as James explains what went wrong.

Rebecca doesn't just offer the standard apology. She goes a step further. "James, I'm really sorry this happened," she says, her voice full of genuine empathy. "I can only imagine how frustrating this must be, especially after a long day. Let me make this right."

And then she does something unexpected: she doesn't just offer to replace the meal. She personally ensures that the correct order is prepared, adds a complimentary dessert as a gesture of goodwill, and arranges for it to be delivered to James's home. Not only that, but she includes a handwritten note with the delivery, saying, "James, we truly appreciate you. Thank you for giving us the chance to make this right."

James, who had been bracing for another frustrating, impersonal interaction, is blown away. Rebecca didn't just correct the mistake—she made him feel important, valued, and heard. The error with his order became irrelevant because the way she handled it made such a profound impression on him. He would return to that restaurant not just because of the food, but because of how Rebecca made him feel.

CUSTOMER SERVICE IS EMOTIONAL INTELLIGENCE IN ACTION

At the heart of every great customer service interaction lies emotional intelligence. The ability to perceive, understand, and manage emotions— both your own and others'—is the key to delivering exceptional service. It's about recognizing that every customer, no matter how routine the interaction might seem, brings with them their own set of feelings, expectations, and needs.

Let's delve deeper.

Consider a father named Ben who has taken the day off work to take hisson, Tommy, to the zoo. It's a special day, one they've been looking forward to for weeks. They arrive early, tickets in hand, ready to see the lions and giraffes. But when they get to the front gate, the ticket scanner malfunctions. The line behind them grows longer, and Tommy, who has been chattering excitedly about the animals, starts to get restless.

The staff member at the gate could have just said, "I'm sorry for the delay.Please wait while we sort this out." But instead, she senses Ben's growing frustration and Tommy's disappointment. So she smiles and says, "I'm so sorry for this little hiccup, Tommy. You must be excited to see the animals, huh? How about this—I'll call someone to help with the tickets, and in the meantime, why don't I give you this zoo map? You can pick out the first animal you want to see, and I'll make sure you and your dad are our VIP guests for the day."

In that moment, the staff member transformed a frustrating situation into a memorable one. She didn't just fix the problem; she connected with Ben and Tommy on an emotional level. Ben no longer felt inconvenienced, and Tommy was over the moon at the idea of being a VIP guest. That's the magic of emotional intelligence in customer service—it's the ability to turn obstacles into opportunities for connection.

CUSTOMER SERVICE AS A PHILOSOPHY, NOT A TASK

At its deepest level, customer service isn't just a role or a task—it's a philosophy. It's a mindset that permeates every interaction, every decision, and every corner of a business. It's the belief that the customer's experience is the foundation of success, that how you make people feel is just as important—if not more so—than the product or service you provide.

Ella's bakery may have grown in size, but its decline came when it lost sight of the philosophy that had built its success in the first place. The bread remained the same, but the connection—the essence of customer service—was no longer front and center. It's a lesson that transcends industries and business sizes: no matter how great your product is, if you neglect the human element, you'll eventually falter.

Maria, the bridal consultant, understood that philosophy. Her job wasn't just to sell dresses; it was to help brides feel seen, heard, and understood. Rebecca, the fast-food manager, embraced that philosophy when she went above and beyond to make James feel valued, even in the face of a mistake. And the zoo staff member? She lived that philosophy when she turned a small ticketing issue into a moment of joy for a father and son.

In the end, customer service is about making people feel good—not just about the product or service they're buying, but about themselves, about their choices, and about the businesses they choose to support. It's about recognizing that every interaction, no matter how small, is an opportunity to make someone's day a little brighter, a little easier, or a little more special.

That is the essence of customer service. It's not just about solving problems or fulfilling requests—it's about creating connections, building trust, and leaving people better than you found them. When you approach customer service with this mindset, you don't just create satisfied customers—you create loyal advocates who will return again and again, not just because of what you offer, but because of how you make them feel.

And that, my friends, is the true power of customer service.

CHAPTER 3: CUSTOMER IS KING

Once upon a time, in a small town nestled between rolling hills and a winding river, there was a humble bakery named "Golden Crust Bakery." This bakery had been passed down through three generations, a legacy that started with Samuel's grandfather, Elijah. Elijah, a craftsman in the art of breadmaking, had opened the bakery on a quiet street corner, his vision simple but profound: a place where everyone could come and experience the best bread, the best pastries, and the warmest of welcomes. His recipe for success wasn't written in any book—it was simply the result of his belief that, no matter what happened, the customer should always feel like royalty when they walked into his shop.

Elijah's son, Samuel's father, took over the bakery when Elijah passed away. While Samuel's father added a few modern touches, like a small café area where people could enjoy freshly baked goods with a cup of coffee, the core philosophy remained unchanged: the customer was alwaysking.

When Samuel inherited the bakery after his father's passing, it wasn't just a business to him. It was the continuation of a family tradition, and more importantly, it was a calling. Samuel loved the bakery, but more than that, he loved the people. He saw his customers as family. And this is where his success began—because, to Samuel, customer service wasn't just a job; it was a way of life.

A HUMBLE BEGINNING

Samuel's bakery wasn't the biggest in town. In fact, there were two other bakeries nearby that were larger, newer, and more modern. They had bigger marketing budgets, flashier signs, and the latest technology. One bakery even had a fancy espresso machine that attracted the young crowd, while the other specialized in gluten-free, vegan pastries that caught the attention of health-conscious foodies.

But what Samuel's bakery had—what no amount of marketing or technology could replicate—was a deep, genuine connection with every person who walked through its doors. Samuel didn't have a fancy loyalty program or an expensive ad campaign. He had something far more valuable: the belief that every customer should feel like a king or queen, whether they were buying a single loaf of bread or a dozen cinnamon rolls.

THE STORY OF CLARA – A CUSTOMER WHO BECAME A FRIEND

One crisp autumn morning, as the leaves fell in golden showers outside the bakery's windows, a young woman named Clara walked through the door. She was new to town, having just moved from a bustling city in search of a fresh start. Life had been tough for Clara. She had recently lost her job in the corporate world, and after months of fruitless searching, she decided to leave the city behind and try her luck in a quieter town. But even in this serene place, Clara still felt lost. The weight of uncertainty hung heavy on her shoulders, and she hadn't yet made any meaningful connections.

Clara hesitated at the counter, glancing at the chalkboard menu but finding herself too distracted to make a decision. Samuel noticed her hesitationimmediately, his eyes narrowing with a gentle concern.

"Good morning!" Samuel greeted her warmly. "What can I get for you today?"

Clara looked up, startled by his friendly voice. "Oh, I'm not sure yet," she mumbled, still uncertain. "I just moved here, and I'm not really hungry. I was just... looking around."

Samuel smiled—a smile that reached his eyes and crinkled the edges of his face. He was used to this—people who wandered in without really knowing what they wanted. Sometimes they needed more than just bread—they needed someone to talk to, someone who would listen, someone who would make them feel seen.

"Well, I can't let you leave without trying something special," Samuel said, his tone playful yet sincere. "How about I make you a fresh croissant and a cup of our finest hot chocolate? It's on the house. Welcome to theneighborhood."

Clara blinked in surprise, looking around at the quiet bakery. "You don't have to do that," she protested, though she was touched by the gesture.

Samuel waved her off, his smile never fading. "No, I insist. It's the least I can do for someone new to town. Besides, it's not every day I get to meeta new neighbor."

A little reluctantly, Clara agreed, and within minutes,

Samuel placed a warm croissant on a plate before her, along with a steaming mug of rich, velvety hot chocolate. The moment Clara took a bite of the croissant, she felt something inside her shift. The pastry was light and flaky, with a buttery richness that danced on her tongue. It was as if the warmth of the bakery wrapped around her and comforted her in a way she hadn't expected.

"You know," Samuel said, pulling up a chair next to her, "there's nothing like a good pastry to make you feel at home."

Clara smiled weakly, feeling a lump form in her throat. For the first time in days, she felt a little lighter. It wasn't just the pastry—it was the kindness in Samuel's eyes, the fact that he had noticed her when no oneelse had.

As the days passed, Clara became a regular at Samuel's bakery. She foundherself looking forward to the mornings she could spend at the bakery, sipping hot chocolate and nibbling on pastries while Samuel asked about her job search, her life, her dreams. He never treated her as a customer; he treated her as a friend—someone he genuinely cared about.

THE SECRET TO SAMUEL'S SUCCESS

It wasn't just Clara. Everyone who came into Samuel's bakery left withmore than they came in for. They left with a feeling of being valued, of being important. Samuel's bakery wasn't a place where you simply bought goods—it was a place where you experienced something more. It was where you felt like you mattered.

People in the town began to notice the difference. They

noticed the care Samuel put into everything he did—the way he greeted every customer by name, the way he remembered their preferences, the way he took the time to ask how they were doing. It wasn't just about selling a loaf of bread—it was about building relationships.

Samuel's competitors noticed, too. They watched as people flocked to Samuel's bakery, as loyal customers returned time and time again, while they struggled to keep up. They tried everything—advertisements, new products, fancy designs—but something was missing. They didn't understand what Samuel understood: that the secret to building a successful business wasn't in what you sold, but in how you made people feel.

THE DAY SAMUEL WALKED MR. THOMPSON HOME

One of the most telling examples of Samuel's philosophy came on a cold winter's day, when an elderly man named Mr. Thompson came into thebakery. Mr. Thompson was a regular—a kind old man who always ordered a single loaf of Samuel's signature sourdough bread. But today, something was different. Mr. Thompson, usually so sprightly, looked frail and tired. He leaned heavily on his cane as he shuffled up to the counter.

"Mr. Thompson, are you alright?" Samuel asked, concern creeping into
his voice.

"Oh, I'm just getting old, Samuel," Mr. Thompson replied with a weak smile. "These old bones aren't what they used to be."

Samuel didn't think twice. He immediately wrapped the sourdough in a cloth, grabbed his coat, and offered, "Let me walk you home today, Mr. Thompson. It's too cold for you to be out here by yourself."

Mr. Thompson protested, but Samuel was insistent. "It's no trouble at all. We'll get you home safely."

And so, Samuel walked Mr. Thompson all the way to his house, chatting with him along the way. When they arrived at Mr. Thompson's door, Samuel made sure the elderly man got inside and was settled before he left. Over the next few weeks, Samuel continued to check on Mr. Thompson regularly, delivering bread to his house and making sure he had everything he needed.

Samuel's actions weren't about marketing or customer service tactics.
They were about genuine care for another person.

THE TRUE COST OF GOODWILL

As the days and weeks passed, a remarkable transformation began to take place in the town. Word of Samuel's extraordinary kindness and the unique atmosphere he had cultivated in his bakery began to spread far and wide. What had once been a small, modest shop, known only to the locals who passed by its welcoming door, soon became a gathering place, a hub of warmth and connection. The bakery, with its humble yet inviting ambiance, was no longer just a place to buy bread. It had become a sanctuary for the soul, where the simple act of purchasing a loaf or a pastry was infused with a deep sense of belonging.

People from all walks of life—young and old, families and individuals—found themselves drawn to Samuel's bakery. They weren't just coming for the freshly baked goods that filled the air with their tantalizing aroma, nor were they merely seeking the convenience of a local bakery. What brought them back, time and again, was the undeniable warmth that emanated from Samuel himself, from his every word, every smile, every gesture. Samuel had an extraordinary gift: the ability to make everyone feel like they were the most important person in the room, that they were seen, heard, and appreciated. It was a rare and precious kind of kindness, one that turned a simple transaction into a meaningful interaction.

The bakery became a place where people not only satisfied their hunger but also found a sense of community. It wasn't just about bread or pastries; it was about the way Samuel took the time to listen to his customers, ask how their day had been, remember their names, and genuinely care about their lives. The exchange of money for goods was almost secondary to the connections being made. Samuel's bakery was alive with conversations, laughter, and the quiet comfort of knowing that you belonged, that you were part of something larger than yourself. It was a space where friendships were forged, where neighbors met and caught up, where families shared stories and created memories.

Despite the growing popularity of Samuel's bakery, the town was soon faced with a new development: another bakery had opened up just down the street. This new bakery, with its sleek, modern design and flashy marketing campaigns, quickly gained attention. It had the kind of polished social media presence that seemed to promise a curated, effortless experience. The exterior boasted gleaming windows and a trendy, Instagram-worthy aesthetic. Inside, the shelves were lined with perfectly uniform pastries, all meticulously arranged and photographed to showcase their "Instagrammable" appeal. It was the kind of bakery you'd expect to see in a bustling metropolis, full of style and sophistication.

On the surface, it appeared that the new bakery had everything going for it—everything, that is, except the one thing that truly mattered. No matter how impressive the new bakery's marketing strategy was, or how well-curated its online presence, it could never replicate the genuine human connection that Samuel had fostered in his own humble establishment. The new bakery might have had the bells and whistles, but it lacked the soul. It was a place where customers were numbers, where transactions were rushed, and where the personal touch was missing entirely. People came in, grabbed their goods, and left—often without so much as a glance or a word to the person behind the counter.

In contrast, Samuel's bakery remained a place of authenticity, a sanctuary that stood apart from the rest. The new bakery might have lured in a few curious customers, but the loyal following that Samuel had built over the years remained steadfast. His customers were not merely patrons—they were his friends, his neighbors, his extended family. And no glossy marketing campaign or trendy design could take away the warmth and the sense of community that radiated from every corner of Samuel's bakery.

There was an undeniable magic in the way Samuel treated his customers, and it was this magic that kept people coming back, time and time again. They didn't just come for the bread, or the pastries, or the coffee; they came for the feeling that Samuel's bakery gave them—a feeling of being seen, of being part of something special. They came for the way they were greeted by name, the way Samuel asked about their families, remembered their birthdays, and listened to their stories. It wasn't just about consuming a product; it was about sharing in the experience of being human, of being connected, and of knowing there was a place where you were always welcome.

In Samuel's bakery, every loaf of bread was baked with care, but it was the relationships that were truly the foundation of his success. It was a place where the essence of community thrived—a place where you weren't just another face in the crowd but a valued and cherished individual. And as time passed, it became clear to everyone that, in the end, it wasn't the flashy marketing or the cutting-edge design that mattered most. It was the heart behind it all—the genuine connection, the warmth, and the unwavering kindness—that made Samuel's bakery a place where people felt at home. It was a place where you didn't just get bread; you got a sense of belonging, a sense of being cared for, and, above all, a sense of love. And that was something no trendy, polished bakery could ever replicate.

THE LEGACY CONTINUES

As Samuel grew older, he began to teach his son, Matthew, the secrets of running the bakery. But there was one lesson that he stressed above all others:

"Matthew, it's never about the product. It's never about how fancy the decor is or how many social media followers we have. It's always about the people. Remember this, son: every person who walks through that door is royalty. Treat them with the respect they deserve. Serve them with your heart, not just your hands. That's the key to success."

Matthew, now grown and fully understanding the gravity of his father's words, took over the bakery as Samuel retired. And just as Samuel had done, Matthew continued the tradition of treating every customer like a king or queen. Because he knew that the customer is always king, and that there is no greater business strategy than a genuine, heartfelt connection.

A FINAL THOUGHT

Samuel's story is a testament to a simple but powerful truth: in business, the customer is indeed king. When we begin to see our customers not as numbers or transactions but as people—people with stories, struggles, and dreams—everything changes. We move from merely offering a product to offering an experience, a relationship, a feeling of belonging. And when we treat customers with respect, kindness, and care, they will reward us with their loyalty, their trust, and their word-of-mouth advocacy.

Samuel's legacy is a reminder to all of us that true business success isn't about competing with flashy technology or running a slick marketing campaign—it's about connecting with people, understanding their needs, and serving them with all the warmth and love we can offer. When you treat your customers like royalty, they'll not only come back—they'll bring their friends, and they'll make your business a part of their lives.

That is the true magic of customer service: customer is king—and kings and queens never forget those who treat them with honor.

CHAPTER 4: NO CUSTOMER, NOBUSINESS

There is an unshakable truth in the world of business, one that every entrepreneur, business owner, and corporate leader must eventually confront: Without customers, there is no business.

This is not just a catchy phrase or a marketing slogan. It is the foundational principle that holds up the entire structure of commerce. Without the steady stream of customers who are willing to pay for the products or services that you provide, there is no revenue. Without revenue, there is no payroll, no growth, no innovation, no future. In fact, without customers, you are not a business—you're just a concept with no support, no audience, and no purpose.

It's easy to get lost in the labyrinth of day-to-day operations—the meetings, the strategy sessions, the product launches, the marketing campaigns—but it's critical to remember that everything you do, every strategy you implement, and every decision you make ultimately revolves around one thing: the customer. If you forget this, if you lose sight of this, the repercussions can be swift and irreversible.

To truly understand why customers are everything, let me take you on a journey through the history of one of the most successful businesses in the world—a tale of perseverance, dedication, and the simple, yet profound, truth that no customer, no business.

A TALE FROM THE PAST: MR. MILLER'S BUTCHER SHOP

Let's travel back to a small town, somewhere nestled in the rolling hills of the countryside. It's not a bustling metropolis, and it's not a sleepy little village where nothing ever happens. It's a place somewhere in between, where the rhythm of life is gentle, and where people still believe in the importance of good service and personal relationships. In this town, there was a small butcher shop owned by a man named Mr. Miller.

Mr. Miller wasn't the wealthiest man in town, nor did he have a grand shop with expensive furnishings and sophisticated advertising campaigns. He didn't have a website or a flashy logo. What he did have, however, was something far more valuable than any of those things: he had loyal customers.

Every morning, Mr. Miller would open his shop with a simple greeting, a handshake, and a smile. He knew the names of his customers. He knew what they liked to buy, how they liked their meat prepared, and, most importantly, he cared about them. He didn't just serve food—he built relationships. For years, his customers had come to him not only for their butchered cuts but for his warmth, his generosity, and his commitment to quality.

But one year, things began to change. A new business opened across the street—a large, modern supermarket called FoodMart. FoodMart was the talk of the town. With its gleaming floors, its high-tech checkout systems, and its vast array of food products, it quickly became the go-to destination for everything people needed. The prices were lower, the selection was wider, and the convenience was unparalleled. FoodMart promised everything the small butcher shop could not: fast service, variety, and modernity.

At first, Mr. Miller was unperturbed. He knew that the personal service he provided was irreplaceable. But as weeks went by, he noticed something disturbing. Fewer people were walking into his shop. The regular customers who had once filled his store were now shopping at FoodMart.

The competition was fierce. FoodMart had deep pockets and a powerful marketing engine. They advertised on the radio, ran special promotions, and flooded social media with dazzling images of fresh produce and succulent cuts of meat. The town's residents were drawn to the allure of a one-stop shop. It seemed as though Mr. Miller's humble butcher shop was losing ground.

But, as the months wore on, something unexpected happened.

The very customers who had flocked to FoodMart began trickling back into Mr. Miller's shop. They came not because FoodMart was bad—no, FoodMart was perfectly fine. They came back because, as great as FoodMart was, it lacked something Mr. Miller's shop had in abundance: genuine care.

WHY PEOPLE RETURN TO WHAT FEELS RIGHT

What FoodMart couldn't offer was personal service—the kind of service that made a customer feel like family. A perfect example of this occurred one chilly winter morning when Mrs. Richards, a regular customer of Mr. Miller, came rushing into the shop. She was in a panic.

"I need sausages for a big family dinner tonight," she said, almost breathless. "But the ones I bought from FoodMart are all wrong. They're too fatty, and they're not the right flavor. Can you help me?"

Mr. Miller didn't hesitate. Without batting an eye, he said, "Of course, Mrs. Richards. I'll make them fresh for you, and I'll have them ready inan hour."

Mrs. Richards was stunned. She had already paid for sausages at FoodMart and was feeling frustrated by the inconvenience. But Mr. Miller wasn'tjust offering a product—he was offering a solution. She was not a number or a sale to him. She was someone he cared about, and that made all thedifference.

When Mrs. Richards came back to pick up the sausages, she was more than just impressed. She was touched. Mr. Miller had gone above and beyond not just to fix the error, but to make her feel valued and heard. He had made sure that the sausages were exactly as she wanted, just the right balance of lean meat and seasoning. He had remembered her preferences.

"That's why I'll always come to you, Mr. Miller," she said, her voice full of appreciation. "You don't just sell me meat. You make sure I get exactlywhat I need."

It was a small act, but it had a profound impact. Mrs. Richards told herfriends about her experience, and soon, word spread. Mr. Miller's reputation grew once more—not just for the quality of his meat, but for the quality of the service he provided. FoodMart, for all its glitz and glamour, couldn't offer the same level of personal attention. They couldn't offer that human touch that made customers feel seen and appreciated.

THE TRUTH ABOUT LOSING CUSTOMERS

As Mr. Miller's business gradually began to recover from its initial setbacks, he had a profound realization that would forever alter the way he approached his work. He came to understand that losing a customer wasn'tsimply a matter of losing a sale—it was much more than that. It was a loss that rippled outward, affecting not just the immediate transaction but everything that customer represented: their potential to influence others, the referrals they could bring, the reputation they could build for the business, and the ongoing relationship they could foster. When a customer walks away, they don't just take their money with them—they take their trust, their loyalty, and their power to shape the narrative around your brand.

Every interaction a business has with a customer is an opportunity to leavea lasting impression, one that could extend far beyond the sale itself. Each customer is an ambassador in their own right. Word-of-mouth—the simple act of a person sharing their experience with others—is one of the mostpotent forms of marketing a business can have. It's organic, it's trustworthy, and it's often more valuable than any ad campaign or promotional strategy. A satisfied customer doesn't just walk away quietly; they tell their friends and family, they post about their positive experience on social media, and they champion your business in their communities. They become a conduit for new business, bringing in fresh customers who,too, will begin to form their own impressions and potentially share theirown stories.

The ripple effect of a loyal customer's recommendation can be exponential. It's not just about one transaction or a single endorsement— it's about creating a growing network of connections that extends beyond your immediate reach. When a customer is satisfied, they are a beacon for your business. But when you lose them, you don't just lose the value of their purchase; you lose the vast, untapped potential of future opportunities.

To truly appreciate the weight of this loss, consider the implications of losing a loyal customer who has been with you for years. The moment they decide to leave, they take with them much more than just their current transaction—they walk away with the promise of future sales, the likelihood of repeat visits, and the hope of bringing in new business through referrals. In many ways, a loyal customer is like a living, breathing advertisement. They don't just purchase your product or service— they advocate for it. They become a part of the fabric of your brand, influencing others through their words, actions, and networks.

The loss of such a customer isn't just a small setback. It's an exponential loss, one that grows over time. Each person they could have recommended, each future transaction that will never happen, each conversation they could have had in the community—all of that is lost in an instant when they walk away. It's a loss that extends beyond the immediate moment and spirals outwards, affecting your future revenue, your brand's image, and your ability to build lasting relationships with potential clients.

Let's take a closer look at the story of Jane, a regular customer at a local coffee shop. For years, Jane had been coming to the same café every morning, eagerly anticipating her daily cappuccino. She had developed a friendly rapport with the barista, Dave, who had been making her coffee for as long as she could remember. Dave knew exactly how she liked it: perfectly foamy with just the right sprinkle of cinnamon. Over time, their interactions had evolved beyond mere customer service into something more personal—a genuine friendship built on small moments of kindness, shared smiles, and mutual respect.

To Jane, the coffee shop wasn't just a place to grab a quick caffeine fix; it was a part of her daily routine, a space where she felt known and appreciated. And for Dave, Jane was more than just a customer—she was a friend who trusted him with her morning ritual. Every time she walked through the door, it was a reaffirmation of the connection they had built over the years.

But one fateful morning, everything changed. Jane walked into the café as usual, expecting the comforting familiarity of her favorite barista and her carefully crafted cappuccino. But to her surprise, a new barista was behind the counter. This new employee wasn't unfriendly, but she was rushed, impersonal, and seemed distracted. There was no warm greeting, no acknowledgment of Jane's regularity, no recognition of her order. The cappuccino that Jane had been drinking every day for years was made incorrectly—it was too milky and lacked the cinnamon she loved so much. It was as though everything that had made her morning coffee routine special had been erased in an instant.

Feeling disheartened but not wanting to cause a scene, Jane didn't say anything. She paid for her drink and left, silently disappointed. The next day, instead of returning to the familiar café, she decided to try the coffee shop across the street. The experience there was decent—nothing extraordinary, but it was passable. The coffee was made quickly, the staff was polite, and the atmosphere was clean. It wasn't the same as the old café, but it was enough to satisfy her need for a quick caffeine fix. Overtime, Jane started to frequent the new shop more and more, slowly replacing her old routine with a new one.

And just like that, Jane stopped coming to Dave's coffee shop. It wasn't a dramatic decision, nor was it a conscious act of betrayal. It was simply the result of one small misstep—a single, seemingly insignificant mistake that led her to explore other options. But what Dave and the coffee shop owners didn't realize was that this wasn't just the loss of one customer. It was the beginning of a chain reaction.

As Jane's routine shifted, so did her narrative. She didn't keep her experience to herself—she shared it. She told her friends about the disappointing service, she vented to her colleagues, and she even posted about it on social media. Her story, though small and seemingly insignificant, began to resonate with others. It was a simple tale of a loyal customer feeling let down by an impersonal experience, but it was enough to sway the opinions of others who were considering where to get their morning coffee. Slowly but surely, other potential customers followed Jane's lead, shifting their business to the new coffee shop across the street.

This is the ripple effect of losing a single customer. What seemed like an isolated incident—the loss of one sale—turned into a snowballing effect, causing a steady decline in the original coffee shop's customer base. The loss of Jane wasn't just a minor inconvenience; it was the beginning of a larger loss of trust, loyalty, and future business. As more and more people began to hear Jane's story, they, too, were influenced by her experience. What started as one lost sale quickly transformed into a growing exodus of customers. The brand damage was done, and the café was no longer the go-to spot for a morning pick-me-up.

When you lose a customer, it's not just the immediate revenue you lose— it's the potential to continue building a loyal following, the opportunity for positive word-of-mouth, and the trust you've built over time. Every customer is a thread in the fabric of your business, and when one thread unravels, it threatens to weaken the entire structure. The ripple effect can be far-reaching, extending well beyond what you may initially perceive. Losing a customer may seem like a small setback in the grand scheme of things, but the impact is often much greater than you realize. It's not just about losing a sale—it's about losing everything that customer represents.

WHY CUSTOMERS ARE YOUR MOST IMPORTANT ASSET

In the end, the lesson is clear. No customer, no business.

Your customers are not just a source of income—they are your partners, your allies, and your advocates. Without them, your business would be nothing more than an empty shell. But when you treat them right, when you give them the service and care they deserve, you create a bond that can last a lifetime.

The heart of your business is not your product, your service, or your location. It's the relationship you have with your customers. And it's through that relationship that your business will thrive.

So next time you face a decision, whether it's about pricing, service, or product development, remember one thing:

without customers, you have nothing. Treat them with the respect and care they deserve, and they'll ensure your business is successful for years to come.

Remember: *No customer, no business.*

CHAPTER 5: RULE #1: IF YOU DON'T TAKE CARE OF YOUR CUSTOMERS, SOMEBODY ELSE WILL

It's a crisp morning in early spring. You've just opened the doors of your newly renovated café, an oasis in the heart of your bustling neighborhood. The rich aroma of freshly brewed coffee swirls around the space, mixing with the warmth of freshly baked pastries. You've meticulously chosen every detail—artisan furniture, calming colors, a playlist of soothing melodies in the background. Every aspect of the atmosphere has been crafted to perfection. You feel a sense of pride as the door chimes ring and the first customers step inside. Today is going to be a great day.

Your first customer of the morning is a young professional, wearing a sleek business suit and a well-practiced smile. She walks up to the counter and orders a cappuccino with an extra shot of espresso, her go-to drink on the go. The barista behind the counter, a young woman with a warm smile, gets to work right away, grinding the beans and preparing the milk with practiced precision. But just as the milk begins to froth, the machine sputters and coughs, producing a strange, uneven foam. The barista fumbles with it, trying to salvage the situation, but it's clear something's gone wrong.

The young woman, initially patient, starts to shift her weight uncomfortably. She checks her watch. The cappuccino isn't arriving quickly enough. And while the barista rushes to fix the issue, there's no communication. No acknowledgment of the delay, no apology, no offer to make it right. The customer's impatience grows. She taps her fingers on the counter, looking around at the other customers who are being served with ease. Finally, after what seems like an eternity, the cappuccino arrives. But it's not quite right. The foam is uneven, the espresso shot too strong. It's not the perfect cup she had hoped for.

She takes a sip, her face showing her disappointment. It's not the worstcup of coffee she's ever had, but it's far from the experience she was expecting. Without a word, she gathers her things and leaves. As she exits the café, she reaches into her bag, pulls out her phone, and leaves a review:"Coffee was good, but the service was slow and unprofessional. I'll probably try the café down the street next time."

The review isn't scathing, but it's enough. That one interaction, that one missed opportunity, could have a lasting impact on your business. You spent months building a beautiful space, crafting the perfect menu, and investing in quality ingredients. Yet, in that single moment, you lost a customer. And not just a customer—but someone who might have been a regular, someone who could have spread the word about how wonderful your café was.

This is the reality of business today. Every interaction with a customer is an opportunity. An opportunity to build a relationship. An opportunity to foster loyalty. An opportunity to make a lasting impression. But when you fail to meet expectations, when you miss the mark even slightly, that opportunity slips away, often never to return. And worse, your competitor—who's ready to provide a better experience—swoops in to steal what should have been yours.

THE POWER OF THE CUSTOMER EXPERIENCE

In the world of business, we often talk about "customer service" as if it's just another task to be managed. We schedule it into our training sessions, we create scripts for employees to follow, and we check off boxes to ensure that everything is "handled." But customer service isn't just a task. It's the very lifeblood of your business. It's what keeps customers coming back. It's what turns a one-time visitor into a loyal fan. It's what keeps your business afloat when the competition is fierce and the margins arethin.

To understand the true power of customer service, you have to shift your perspective. Think of your business as more than just a place that provides a product or service. Think of it as a hub for building relationships. Each time a customer interacts with you, they're not just buying a product—they're entering into an experience. How that experience unfolds will determine whether they stay or go, whether they return with friends or leave without a second thought.

Let me take you to the story of Cleo's Bookstore, a small, independent bookstore that had been operating in a busy metropolitan area for years.Cleo, the owner, had always prided herself on creating a space where people could not only buy books but escape into another world. She had carefully curated her selection, adding everything from popular bestsellers to obscure gems that would make even the most discerning bibliophile's heart flutter.

But while Cleo had a beautiful store, it wasn't enough. Her competitors were large chain bookstores with bigger inventories and deeper pockets. The market was becoming increasingly difficult to navigate, and Cleo knew something had to change.

It was during a particularly slow afternoon that Cleo had an epiphany. As she sat behind the counter, a regular customer named Rachel came in. Rachel was a college professor who often visited Cleo's store during her lunch break. Cleo knew that Rachel always had a keen interest in historical novels and obscure philosophy texts. Today, however, Rachel seemed distracted, scanning the shelves with a somewhat defeated expression.

"Is everything alright, Rachel?" Cleo asked as she greeted her with a smile.

Rachel sighed and replied, "I'm just so tired of ordering the same books over and over from the big stores. They've got everything I need, but it feels impersonal, you know? I can't tell if anyone there even cares about what I like."

In that moment, Cleo realized what she was missing. She wasn't just selling books—she was selling an experience. An experience where customers didn't just buy something off the shelf, but felt seen, heard, and valued. From that day on, Cleo made a concerted effort to engage with each of her customers. She learned their tastes, remembered their preferences, and made sure to recommend books that they would truly enjoy. When a new shipment of books arrived, Cleo made sure to notify her regulars first, inviting them to come in and take a look before the rest of the crowd. She even started offering personalized book suggestions based on her customers' individual tastes.

It didn't take long for Cleo's Bookstore to become a neighborhood institution. Word of mouth spread, and her loyal customers started bringing in friends and family. People didn't just come for the books—they came for the experience. They came for Cleo's attention, her care, and her dedication to creating a community of readers who felt appreciated. Cleo didn't just sell books; she sold an experience they couldn't get anywhere else. And that's what made all the difference.

WHY CUSTOMERS LEAVE

Now, you might be thinking, "That's great, but I don't have the time or resources to offer such personalized service." Let's be real: many businesses feel the pressure of time, staff shortages, and the demands of day-to-day operations. But the truth is, the level of care and attention you give to your customers doesn't have to be grandiose. It doesn't have to be elaborate. It just has to be genuine.

The moment you stop paying attention to the details, however, is the moment you start losing customers. People don't leave because you made one mistake; they leave because they feel neglected. They leave because their experience didn't match their expectations. They leave because, over time, they didn't feel valued.

Consider Lori's Bridal Boutique, a high-end shop specializing in wedding dresses. Lori had always prided herself on offering personalized, one-on-one consultations with brides. She would spend hours with each client, helping them find the perfect dress for their big day. But over time, Lori got overwhelmed. As her business grew, she hired more staff, and the personalized touch she had become known for started to slip away. The consultants were trained to push sales, but they didn't spend the time getting to know the brides. There were long waits, rushed appointments, and a sense that the customer wasn't the priority.

One bride, Sarah, had been dreaming of her wedding dress for years. She came into Lori's Boutique, hoping for the same experience that her friends had raved about. Unfortunately, what she encountered was the opposite. Her consultant barely spoke to her, didn't ask about her wedding plans, and seemed distracted throughout the appointment. The dresses she was shown didn't fit her vision at all. After trying on several gowns that didn't feel "right," Sarah left, disappointed and frustrated.

Later, Sarah found another boutique, one that offered the same beautiful dresses, but where the staff took the time to listen. They asked about her wedding, her dreams, her vision. They made sure she felt special, guiding her through the process with genuine care and attention. In the end, Sarah said yes to the dress—and more importantly, she became a loyal customer who would share her positive experience with others. Lori's Boutique, unfortunately, lost out because they failed to take care of their customers. They didn't value the emotional experience that comes with choosing a wedding dress.

THE REAL COST OF LOSING CUSTOMERS

When you fail to take care of your customers, it's not just about losing one sale. It's about losing the long-term trust of an individual who could have been a brand ambassador for your business. One customer has the potential to influence dozens of others through word of mouth, online reviews, and social media. And when you lose that trust, you lose not just the person, but the ripple effect that follows.

The truth is, in today's hyperconnected world, a single negative experience can reverberate far beyond what you might imagine. Consider the story of Dave's Diner, a small but beloved local restaurant. For years, Dave's Diner had been the go-to place for families, students, and workers who craved a warm meal and friendly service. However, as the restaurant grew in popularity, something began to slip. The staff got busier, the kitchen struggled to keep up, and the personal touch Dave had once offered seemed to fade into the background.

One night, a regular customer named Jenny came in with her family. The restaurant was packed, and Jenny had to wait longer than usual to be seated. When she was finally shown to a table, she noticed that the table wasn't cleaned properly. The silverware was smudged, and the menu was covered in stains. As she waited for her meal, she overheard a waiter complaining about how hard it was to keep up with orders. Jenny, feeling ignored and uncomfortable, decided to leave. Before she left, she posted a quick review: "Used to love this place, but the service has gone downhill. I'm not sure if I'll be coming back."

The next morning, Jenny's review was shared by her followers, and soon enough, others chimed in with similar experiences. Dave's Diner, once a staple in the community, began to see a steady decline in customers. The problem wasn't the food—it was the experience. And in the restaurant industry, where competition is fierce and customers have so many options, the experience is everything.

HOW TO TAKE CARE OF YOUR CUSTOMERS

So, how do you avoid these pitfalls and ensure your customers always feel valued? Here are some practical ways to make sure your customers never feel neglected:

• **Be Present:** Whether it's online or in person, make sure you're actively engaging with your customers. Respond to inquiries promptly, acknowledge their presence, and make sure they feel heard.

• **Set Realistic Expectations:** Be transparent about wait times, potential delays, and any other challenges your business may face. Customers appreciate honesty and will be more understanding if they know what to expect.

• **Personalize the Experience:** As Cleo did at her bookstore, take the time to get to know your customers. Remember their preferences and offer tailored recommendations that show you care.

• **Go Above and Beyond:** Don't just meet expectations—exceed them. Offer little surprises, like a free drink for a loyal customer or a handwritten thank-you note with a purchase. It's these small gestures that can have a big impact.

• **Train Your Team:** Make sure your team understands the importance of customer care. Train them to engage with customers, solve problems quickly, and always put the customer first.

• **Follow Through:** If you promise something— whether it's a service or a product—make sure you deliver. Follow up with customers to ensure they're satisfied with their experience, and be quick to address any issues.

• **Value Feedback:** Always listen to your customers.

Encourage reviews and pay attention to both positive and negative feedback. Use this information to improve and grow your business.

CONCLUSION

The reality is this: If you don't take care of your customers, somebody elsewill. Whether you're running a café, a bookstore, a boutique, or any other business, the fundamental principle remains the same. Your customers are the heartbeat of your business. Without them, there is no business.

Take care of them. Value them. Understand them. And in doing so, you'll not only keep them coming back—you'll build a reputation that will last for years to come. Because at the end of the day, the businesses that succeed are the ones that remember this rule: Customer care isn't optional.It's essential.

CHAPTER 6: HOW TO INTRODUCE AND ADVERTISE YOUR PRODUCT

The moment you bring a new product to life is an exhilarating one. It's akin to a painter standing in front of a blank canvas, or a chef unveiling a new recipe to an eager audience—it's a point of origin, an intersection of vision and reality. But just as the journey to creating a product is full of steps and challenges, so too is the road to introducing and advertising it. The way you introduce and advertise your product has the power to make or break its success. If done correctly, you don't just launch a product—you build a movement, create an experience, and form an emotional bond between your brand and your customers.

Let's take a deep dive into the intricacies of how to introduce and advertise your product. To help illustrate the process, I want to share the story of a small, yet incredibly successful, local coffee shop that mastered the art of product launch and advertising—a story that teaches us not only about strategy but about how to connect with customers on a deeper level.

A CASE STUDY: THE COFFEE SHOP THAT TURNED A PRODUCT LAUNCH INTO A STORY

Sarah, the owner of "Brewed Awakening," a family-owned coffee shop nestled in the heart of a bustling city, was preparing for a major new product launch. She had just developed a new line of specialty, gourmet coffee blends, and she was eager to introduce them to her customers. But Sarah knew the stakes were high—she wasn't just launching a new product; she was introducing a transformation to her customers' coffee-drinking habits. She knew that in today's crowded marketplace, it wasn't enough to simply put a product on the shelves and hope for the best. She had to advertise it in a way that was compelling, memorable, and capable of creating deep customer loyalty.

Let me walk you through the steps Sarah took—and the lessons we can all learn from her journey.

STEP 1: UNDERSTAND YOUR PRODUCT AND YOUR AUDIENCE

Sarah's first step was perhaps the most fundamental, yet often overlooked: she took the time to truly understand her product. She didn't just slap a label on the new coffee blends and call it a day. She took pride in knowing what made her coffee unique. She studied the beans' origins, the process by which they were grown, harvested, roasted, and blended. She understood every facet of her product—from the taste profile to the impact on the environment and local communities. But that wasn't all. She understood her customers deeply.

In the world of advertising, understanding your audience is paramount. You can have the best product in the world, but if you fail to understand the needs, desires, and pain points of your audience, you'll struggle to make an impact. Sarah's customers were not just people who drank coffee—they were people who savored the ritual of brewing a cup, who valued the artistry behind the perfect blend, and who cared about the source of their beans.

As Sarah prepared to introduce the new line, she spent weeks meeting withher regulars, conducting informal interviews, and taking surveys. What were her customers craving? What were their frustrations with the current coffee options on the market? Did they care about sustainability? Did they prefer single-origin coffee? These were the questions that fueled her understanding of the market.

By the time the new blends were ready for launch, Sarah not only knew everything there was to know about the coffee but had also built a clear customer profile. Her customers were passionate about quality, ethically sourced products, and they craved novelty in their daily coffee experience.

ACTIONABLE TIP:

Before introducing your own product, immerse yourself in both the product and the market. Ask yourself questions like:

- What need does this product fulfill?
- Who exactly will benefit from it?
- Why is this product important to them?

By answering these questions, you will be armed with the knowledge you need to speak to your audience in a meaningful way.

STEP 2: BUILD A COMPELLING NARRATIVE

Sarah didn't just want to tell her customers that her coffee was "better" than what they were used to. She wanted to make them feel like they were becoming part of something larger. She wanted her customers to not just enjoy the coffee, but to believe in the story behind it. A product narrative isn't just a marketing tool—it's a powerful way to connect emotionally with your audience and distinguish yourself from the competition.

Sarah took her customers on a journey. She shared how she had traveled to Colombia to meet the farmers who grew the beans she was now offering. She spoke about the farmers' dedication to sustainable practices and their commitment to improving their communities. Sarah told her customers that each sip of coffee wasn't just a delicious experience; it was a taste of the farmers' labor, care, and culture. She made it clear that each bag of coffee came with a story, a purpose, and a reason for being.

Through storytelling, Sarah didn't just market her product; she invited her customers to become part of her brand's mission. When she launched the new coffee line, it wasn't simply a transactional exchange; it was a community-building event. She framed her new product as a means of supporting global sustainability efforts, a way of contributing to a

movement of ethical consumption, and a small step toward making a larger difference in the world.

ACTIONABLE TIP:

Think about your product's story. Why does it exist? What makes it different from what's already out there? What journey will your customers embark on when they purchase it? Craft a narrative that not only informs but also inspires.

STEP 3: CREATE A SENSE OF URGENCY

The art of product advertising lies not just in its message but in its timing. Sarah knew that in order to truly get people's attention, she had to create a sense of urgency—without it, her gourmet coffee blends would simply blend into the crowd. She couldn't afford to be just another coffee shop in the city. She needed her product to stand out, and she needed her customers to act quickly.

Sarah didn't just launch her new coffee line on a random Wednesday. She planned a grand opening event—a launch party that promised an exclusive experience. She invited customers to a VIP tasting event where they would be the first to try the blends, meet the farmers, and learn about the sustainable farming practices. But she didn't stop there. She also offered a limited-time discount for early buyers and promoted the idea that these coffee blends would only be available in limited quantities.

She understood that people hate to miss out. When you create a sense of scarcity and exclusivity, you push people to act now. "If I don't buy it today, will it be gone tomorrow?" becomes a powerful motivator.

ACTIONABLE TIP:

Think about how you can create urgency for your own product. Limited-time offers, early-bird discounts, and exclusive events can all play a role in pushing your audience to take action immediately.

STEP 4: USE SOCIAL PROOF TO BUILD TRUST

Sarah understood one of the most powerful truths about advertising: people trust their peers more than they trust brands. If someone else says something is worth buying, we are far more likely to act on it. This is where social proof comes in.

She carefully selected a group of her loyal customers and asked them to try the new coffee before the launch. She didn't just want their opinion; she wanted them to become brand advocates. She then encouraged them to share their experiences on social media—posting pictures of their coffee cups, writing about their favorite blends, and sharing what made the coffee so special.

This strategy didn't just rely on Sarah's word. Instead, it amplified the voices of the customers who were already passionate about the coffee, turning them into organic marketers. People began tagging the coffee shop in their posts, sharing their experiences, and spreading the excitement.

Social proof is a powerful tool because it builds trust. People are more likely to believe that your product is valuable if they see others enjoying it. This validation from peers often converts passive interest into actual purchases.

ACTIONABLE TIP:

Leverage your satisfied customers to create social proof. Ask for reviews, testimonials, and user-generated content. The more people speak about your product, the more legitimate and trustworthy it becomes.

STEP 5: UTILIZE MULTIPLE ADVERTISING CHANNELS

Sarah understood that modern advertising requires a multi-channel approach. No single advertising strategy would reach everyone, and so she made sure to spread her message far and wide.

She used social media to showcase beautiful photos of her new coffee blends. Instagram became a key platform for her, where she posted eye-catching images of her coffee, behind-the-scenes stories, and customer testimonials. Facebook allowed her to engage directly with her audience, answering questions and building community.

But Sarah didn't just rely on social media. She also sent personalized email campaigns to her existing customers. These emails not only announced the launch but also offered an exclusive early-bird discount to her loyal patrons. She ran paid ads on Google to target coffee enthusiasts in the local area and even collaborated with food bloggers to increase visibility.

By leveraging multiple platforms—social media, email, paid ads, influencer partnerships, and in-store promotions—Sarah ensured that her message reached her customers wherever they were. She wasn't relying on just one channel to carry the weight; she made sure her advertising campaign had multiple touchpoints to keep her brand top of mind.

ACTIONABLE TIP:

Use a mix of channels to introduce and advertise your product. Think about where your target audience spends their time—whether it's on social media, in email inboxes, or through word-of-mouth—and be present in those spaces.

STEP 6: ENGAGE AND FOLLOW UP FOR LONG-TERM SUCCESS

The launch is just the beginning. Sarah knew that if she wanted her new coffee blends to become a long-term success, she needed to continue building on the momentum she had created. She didn't just launch the product and disappear. She engaged with her customers, asked for feedback, and adjusted her strategies based on their responses. She invited them back for "coffee of the month" events and offered new promotions based on their preferences.

Sarah also invested in building a relationship with her customers by consistently delivering exceptional experiences. She personalized her communications, offering tailored recommendations based on individual preferences.

By staying connected, Sarah not only kept her customers engaged but also ensured that they would become repeat buyers. The emotional connection she cultivated ensured her product wasn't just a one-time purchase; it became an ongoing experience that customers continued to seek out.

ACTIONABLE TIP:

Don't let the excitement of your product launch fade away. Keep engaging with your customers and, most importantly, listen to their feedback. Continue to nurture the relationships you've built, and you'll see lasting success.

In conclusion, introducing and advertising a product is more than just about making a sale. It's about creating a story that connects emotionally with your audience, building trust through social proof, leveraging multiple advertising channels, and fostering long-term relationships with your customers. If you can master these steps and truly understand both your product and your audience, you'll be well on your way to making a lasting impact in the market.

CHAPTER 7: HOW TO ATTRACT CUSTOMERS

Attracting customers is not just about advertising your product or service in a catchy way. It's not simply about offering discounts or having a flashy online presence. True customer attraction is about creating something that resonates deeply with people. It's about crafting an experience, telling a compelling story, and building a relationship based on trust. It's about transforming the transactional nature of business into a personal connection.

To understand the intricacies of attracting customers, let's dive into a tale that might seem simple on the surface, but holds deep lessons for any entrepreneur—whether you're just starting out or looking to take your business to the next level. This is the story of Lena's Coffee House, a small, unassuming café on a quiet street corner. By the end of this chapter, you will see that there's much more to Lena's success than just the coffee she served.

THE HUMBLE BEGINNING OF LENA'S COFFEE HOUSE

Lena's Coffee House was located in a charming neighborhood, where ablend of old-town charm and modern-day hustle merged seamlessly. But the café was easy to overlook at first—its signage was simple, and its storefront was modest. Inside, the ambiance wasn't loud or imposing; it was comfortable, welcoming, and cozy, much like the old-fashioned parlors where you could sit for hours and have deep, thoughtful conversations over a hot cup of tea. The place didn't scream "come here" with flashy lights or over-the-top promotions. And yet, despite its low-key appeal, it became one of the most sought-after spots in town.

How did this happen? How did a small, local business with no large marketing budget manage to attract such a loyal following? The answerlies in the way Lena approached the whole idea of customer attraction. Shedidn't simply aim to sell coffee; she aimed to create a community, to nurture relationships, and to build a brand that was about more than just the products it offered.

It all started with a shift in perspective: Lena knew that to attract customers, she had to deeply understand them, their needs, desires, andemotional triggers.

She realized that attracting customers is about more than just appealing to their desire for products or services—it's about creating a space for connection, where people feel like they belong. And this was exactly what Lena did: she created a space of belonging.

STEP 1: UNDERSTAND YOUR CUSTOMERS— THEIR NEEDS, WANTS, AND ASPIRATIONS

Every business, big or small, must start by understanding its audience. This might seem like a no-brainer, but in many cases, businesses overlook the importance of truly knowing their customers. In Lena's case, she didn't just want to sell coffee to people who happened to walk by. She wanted to know her customers—not just by their names, but by their stories, what they cared about, and what they sought when they walked through her door. She spent hours observing and engaging with her customers. This might seem tedious, but it was the key to her success.

Lena was intentional in the way she approached customer interactions. She knew that people came to her café for more than just a caffeine fix—they came for the experience. She knew that some customers came because they were looking for a quiet place to work or study. Others came to meet friends, network, or simply escape the pressures of the world. A few came because they were artists looking for inspiration, and still, others came for the warmth of human connection. Lena understood these nuances, and she used this knowledge to craft a customer experience that met those needs at every touchpoint.

Think about your own business. Do you know why your customers come to you? Do you understand their deepest desires? This is crucial, because attracting customers starts with understanding what they value most—whether it's a specific problem you solve, an emotional need you meet, or a desire for a product that makes their life better.

STEP 2: CRAFT AN IRRESISTIBLE EXPERIENCE—NOT JUST A PRODUCT

The next step in attracting customers is to craft an experience. Lena knew she wasn't just selling coffee; she was offering an atmosphere, a moment in time, and a feeling of connection. That was the magic of her café—it wasn't about just serving a cup of coffee; it was about serving an experience that customers would remember, something they couldn't get elsewhere. Every customer that walked through the door was treated not as a transaction, but as a guest.

Take a moment to think about your business. Are you just selling a product or service, or are you offering an experience? When people walk into your store or visit your website, what do they feel? What kind of memories do you want them to leave with? Every step of the customer journey—whether in person or online—should be meticulously designed to offer a memorable experience.

Lena's café wasn't just a place where coffee was served—it was a haven. A place where the baristas didn't just hand over a cup of coffee; they smiled, greeted customers by name, and made them feel like they belonged. It was a place where the music set the perfect ambiance, where the furniture was arranged to encourage conversation, and where the walls were decorated with the works of local artists. These little details might seem insignificant, but they made all the difference in creating a memorable experience.

The most successful businesses are those that know how to surprise and delight their customers at every turn. From the moment they engage with your brand, to the point they leave, every interaction should leave them feeling valued and appreciated. Whether it's through the warmth of your customer service or the quality of your product, customers are more likely to return if they feel like they've been part of something unique, something memorable.

STEP 3: BUILD RELATIONSHIPS AND ESTABLISH TRUST

Attracting customers is not a one-time event—it's a long-term relationship. One of the most powerful lessons from Lena's story is that the business-owner-customer relationship must be built on trust.

Every customer who walked into Lena's Coffee House knew they could count on two things: first, that their coffee would be served with the same care and excellence every time, and second, that Lena would remember their name and treat them like a person, not just a sale. She didn't just take orders—she had conversations. She asked people about their day, their families, their creative projects. She took the time to truly connect with them on a personal level.

Trust is the foundation of any relationship, and it's the same with your customers. If your customers trust you, they'll return. They'll become loyal advocates for your brand. They'll spread the word about how much they value your business, and they'll invite others to join in. Trust is built over time—through consistent service, reliability, and personal care. Lena didn't offer the cheapest coffee in town, nor did she have the largest menu, but she delivered on her promises every time. Her customers knew that they could rely on her for an exceptional experience, and that's why they kept coming back.

In your own business, building trust involves consistently delivering high-quality products or services and treating customers with respect you're your customers see that you are trustworthy, they'll be more likely to return—and bring others with them.

STEP 4: USE THE POWER OF STORYTELLING TOCONNECT EMOTIONALLY

Humans are natural storytellers. We connect with stories in ways that facts and figures can't match. Lena knew this and understood the profound impact that storytelling can have on building customer loyalty. She didn't just market her café as a place to grab a cup of coffee; she shared storiesof how the café was founded, how she connected with the local community, and how she worked tirelessly to bring people together through art, coffee, and conversation.

Storytelling isn't just for marketing—it's a tool for connecting with your audience on a deep emotional level. When customers hear your story, they want to be a part of it. They want to be involved in something bigger than just a transaction. They want to know the person behind the brand. They want to know the why behind the what. This is where the magic happens.

Lena's story resonated with her customers because it was authentic. People love to support businesses that are built on passion, authenticity, and purpose. The more you share your story—the reason why you do what you do—the more your customers will feel connected to your brand. They'll begin to see themselves in your story, and in turn, they'll become loyal followers and advocates.

STEP 5: HARNESS THE POWER OF SOCIAL PROOF

In today's digital world, one of the most powerful tools you can use to attract customers is social proof. Lena's café didn't just rely on word ofmouth; she actively encouraged her customers to share their experiences online. They posted photos of their drinks, shared stories about their favorite moments at the café, and tagged Lena's Coffee House in their social media posts.

This is the essence of social proof—the idea that people are influenced by the actions and opinions of others. We trust the recommendations of our peers more than traditional advertising, and this is especially true in today's age of social media.

Lena wasn't just relying on advertising to attract customers—she was using her customers as her best marketing tool. By encouraging social media engagement and fostering a sense of community, Lena tapped into a powerful form of marketing. The more people posted about their experiences, the more exposure the café received. Word spread like wildfire, and soon, people from all over the city were traveling to Lena's Coffee House, eager to experience the place for themselves.

STEP 6: USE DIGITAL MARKETING TO EXPANDYOUR REACH

In Lena's case, she was able to attract customers both locally and from afar by embracing digital marketing. She used social media platforms like Instagram, Facebook, and Twitter to share the story of her café, connectwith her customers, and keep them updated about events, promotions, and new offerings. Through these platforms, Lena could engage with her customers on a personal level, answer their questions, and foster a sense of community.

Digital marketing isn't just about pushing ads to your audience. It's about creating a conversation. It's about building relationships, engaging with your audience, and sharing content that matters. Content marketing, whether it's through blog posts, videos, or social media, should always aim to connect with customers emotionally. When you engage with your customers in an authentic, transparent way, you not only attract them— you build trust.

STEP 7: FOSTER A SENSE OF EXCLUSIVITY

Humans have a natural desire to feel special. We want to be part of something unique, something that not everyone has access to. This is why Lena created a sense of exclusivity within her café. Whether it was through members-only events, secret menu items, or limited-edition coffee blends, she made her loyal customers feel like they were part of an exclusive club.

This sense of exclusivity was powerful because it made her customers feel valued. When people feel like they belong to something special, they are more likely to return and bring others with them. The key is to offer value without creating a sense of elitism—make people feel special, not excluded.

CONCLUSION

Attracting customers is a journey. It's about creating a space for connection, building relationships, and offering an experience that resonates deeply with people. It's about understanding your customers, telling your story, and leveraging the power of social proof, digital marketing, and exclusivity to build a loyal customer base. Just as Lena transformed her humble coffee shop into a beloved community hub, you too can attract customers who are not just buying your products—they are joining your journey.

CHAPTER 8: HOW TO BUILD A BRAND & A GOOD REPUTATION

Building a brand and cultivating a good reputation is not simply about selling a product or service. It's a journey, a transformation, and a lasting legacy that is created over time. Imagine your brand as a living, breathing entity that grows, evolves, and flourishes. To construct something meaningful, it requires careful planning, deliberate actions, and the passion to back it all up. This chapter will take you deep into the intricate and often overlooked process of creating a brand and reputation that standsthe test of time.

In this chapter, we will explore how to create a brand from the ground up. We will see how vision, authenticity, consistency, reputation-building, and customer connection all play integral roles in the process. I want you to imagine that this journey is not just for a business, but for any individualor organization that wishes to build something that reflects their deepest values and aspirations. A great brand is more than a logo; it's the embodiment of who you are, what you stand for, and why people should care. It's about creating something that people are proud to be associated with, and something that resonates with their core beliefs.

THE GENESIS OF A BRAND

Let's start by considering the early days of a business—just like any new relationship, the beginning is often the hardest. You have an idea, you have energy, and you have a spark of excitement, but you don't have a brand yet. Without a brand, your business is a collection of products or services without a clear identity. It's like a person with no name, no face, no personality. And while you may have a great product, if no one knows whoyou are or what you represent, it's easy to get lost in the noise.

Take, for example, Emma and David, a couple who launched a small startup after months of dreaming and planning. They had a great product that they were passionate about—a product that could change people's lives—but there was one problem: no one knew who they were. No oneknew their story, and no one understood what they were about. They realized that simply having a great product was not enough. They needed to build something bigger, something that could connect emotionally with people, something that could stand out in a crowded market.

This is the moment when Emma and David had to make a critical decision: they needed to establish a brand, one that resonated with their target audience and that would set them apart from all the competitors in their field. They weren't just going to sell a product—they were going to builda legacy.

THE FIRST STEP

Emma and David's journey began by asking themselves a powerful question: Why do we exist? This is where most entrepreneurs get stuck. They often start by thinking, what do we sell or how can we make money? But the real question should always be: Why does our product or service matter to people? Why does it exist beyond just being something that makes money or fills a need?

They sat down together, their pens poised, their minds open. They began brainstorming about their product, its potential impact, and the deeper meaning behind it. It wasn't just about selling a product—it was about creating a movement. Emma and David realized that their product had the power to improve people's lives, to give them the tools they needed to take control of their own futures.

That realization—that their product was more than just an item on a shelf, but a catalyst for change—became the cornerstone of their brand. They would build their brand around this core belief: *empowering individuals to better themselves, one product at a time.*

CRAFTING YOUR STORY

Once Emma and David had their "why," it was time to build the story that would embody it. A brand is nothing without a story—this story becomes the guiding light that illuminates every action, decision, and communication. It becomes the heartbeat of your business. A brand story isn't just a tagline or a mission statement; it's the narrative of your company's origins, its struggles, its victories, and its promise for the future. It's what makes your business human and relatable.

Emma and David knew they couldn't just make claims about their product—they needed to show how their journey reflected the values they were trying to sell. They weren't selling just another product; they were selling a transformation. They began to write their brand story, from the first spark of the idea to the countless hours spent in their garage, perfecting their product, to the challenges they faced and overcame together.

Their story was about resilience, passion, and dedication. It was about two people who wanted to make a difference in the world. It was about using their product to give people more than just a solution; they wanted to give them hope, encouragement, and the belief that change was possible. Emma and David's brand story became their blueprint—the compass by which they would navigate every decision.

AUTHENTICITY

One of the most critical elements of building a brand that resonates is authenticity. In a world full of advertisements, gimmicks, and manipulative marketing tactics, people are looking for something real. Consumers are tired of brands that put on a facade. They crave honesty, transparency, and genuine connections. If your brand isn't authentic, people will see through it. They will sense that something is off, and they won't trust you.

For Emma and David, authenticity was at the core of their brand. They weren't interested in pretending to be something they weren't. Their story was real, and their product was real, and they wanted their customers to feel that. Their authenticity wasn't just in the words they spoke; it was reflected in everything they did. It was reflected in the way they communicated with their customers, the way they treated their employees, and the way they responded to feedback.

One particular incident comes to mind. A customer, Sarah, had ordered their product and received it with a minor defect. Most companies would have simply apologized and replaced the item. But Emma and David saw an opportunity to further cement their reputation. They didn't just send a replacement—they personally wrote Sarah a heartfelt letter explaining how much her feedback meant to them, and how they would work to improve their process. They also included a voucher for her next purchase,to show their appreciation.

This small act of transparency and care made a huge impact. Sarah didn't just become a repeat customer—she became an ambassador for their brand. She shared her experience with her friends and family, and soon Emma and David had more customers than they could keep up with. But it wasn't just the product that kept people coming back—it was the brand's authenticity.

CONSISTENCY

You've probably heard the phrase, "Consistency is key," and when it comes to building a brand, it couldn't be truer. Consistency isn't just about having the same logo or using the same colors; it's about maintaining a consistent message, tone, and experience across every single touchpoint with your customers. Whether someone is visiting your website, reading your social media posts, or interacting with your customer service team, they should receive the same brand experience.

For Emma and David, consistency was critical. They made sure that their message was clear, from their website to their emails, to their social media accounts. They used the same tone of voice across all platforms—warm, inviting, and always encouraging. They didn't deviate from their story or their mission, no matter how tempting it was to chase after new trends or try to appeal to a different audience. Their brand was built on their "why," and they remained true to it, no matter what.

Consistency in branding also means delivering on promises. If you promise a certain level of service or product quality, you must deliver it every time. Emma and David understood this. They knew that building trust with their customers meant delivering the same experience, day in and day out. They didn't want to be known for one great experience; they wanted to be known for consistently providing value and exceeding expectations.

REPUTATION

Building a good reputation is the culmination of everything Emma and David did in building their brand. It wasn't just about making a sale or running an ad campaign—it was about creating an ongoing relationship with their customers. They didn't just sell products; they built trust, rapport, and loyalty.

A brand's reputation is built through every interaction, every product, every piece of content, and every customer service experience. It's not about trying to be perfect, but about owning your mistakes and making things right. When things went wrong, Emma and David didn't shy away. They faced the issue head-on, apologized when needed, and went out oftheir way to make things right.

One of their customers, James, had an issue with an order, and although the mistake wasn't their fault, they took the initiative to fix it. They senthim a new product, free of charge, along with a personal note thankinghim for his patience. James was so impressed by the level of care that he posted about it online. His post went viral, and suddenly, Emma and David's brand was gaining attention they hadn't anticipated.

Their reputation grew because they consistently delivered great products, exceptional service, and above all, integrity. People began to trust them, not just because of their product but because of who they were as a company. They were known for doing the right thing, even when it wasn't easy. That reputation became the foundation of their success.

WORD OF MOUTH

While advertising and marketing are essential, word of mouth is still one of the most powerful tools for growing a brand. Emma and David knewthat if they focused on providing exceptional value and building strong relationships, their customers would do the marketing for them. People trust recommendations from friends and family more than they trust advertisements, and Emma and David understood that.

They didn't spend huge sums on paid ads. Instead, they focused on creating great experiences for their customers, which in turn, led to those customers recommending their brand to others. Word of mouth became their best form of advertising, and it was free.

THE LONG JOURNEY TO BRAND SUCCESS

As time passed, Emma and David's brand continued to grow. They expanded their reach, attracted new customers, and gained the loyalty of existing ones. But through it all, they stayed true to their story, their values, and their mission. They were building something that wasn't just about profit; it was about creating an impact that would last. Their brand was no longer just a product—it was a movement, a legacy of trust, authenticity, and commitment to excellence.

Their reputation, built on a foundation of care, authenticity, and consistency, became the driving force behind their success. Their brand wasn't just recognized; it was revered. And as they looked back on theirjourney, they realized that building a brand and a good reputation wasn't just about the product—it was about who they were, how they treated people, and the lasting impact they made on the world.

Their story is one of resilience, dedication, and authenticity—a story that proved that a great brand, one that's built on strong values and a clear vision, can not only survive but thrive. And the best part? The story is just beginning.

CHAPTER 9: HOW TO SELL

Selling is an art. It's a dance. It's not just about pushing a product on someone—it's about guiding them to see how your product or service can make their lives better. Whether it's a service that makes their day easier, a product that brings them joy, or a solution to a problem they didn't even realize they had—selling is about creating a bond of trust and understanding. It's about making the person across from you feel heard, seen, and appreciated, not just as a potential buyer, but as a human being with unique needs, desires, and challenges.

Selling has been a part of human culture for centuries, from ancient marketplaces to modern e-commerce platforms. However, despite the changing times and technologies, the core of selling remains the same: relationships. To sell successfully, you need to build meaningful connections, truly understand your customer's world, and offer them a solution that improves their situation.

I want to share a story with you—a story that changed my entire perspective on sales. It's a story about my good friend, Michael. Michael's journey into sales is one that I'll never forget, because it illustrates something essential about the nature of selling: it's not about the product, it's about the person.

THE STORY OF MICHAEL

Let me take you back to when Michael first started in sales. Michael was smart. He had the knowledge, the drive, and the ambition to succeed. He was in his mid-20s, fresh out of college, and ready to take on the world.He'd landed a job selling vacuum cleaners—a solid commission-based role that promised big rewards for the right person. On paper, it seemed like a perfect fit.

But Michael wasn't having the success he expected. Every day, he'd drive to neighborhoods, knock on doors, and demonstrate the vacuum cleaner. He would show potential customers how the machine worked, highlightits features, and promise them a cleaner, healthier home. But despite his technical prowess, sales were sluggish. He didn't understand why. Theproduct was good. The price was right. He was doing everything the training manuals told him to do—but still, nothing was clicking.

I'll never forget the day he called me, frustrated. "I just don't get it," hesaid. "I'm doing everything they said to do, but I'm still not closing enoughdeals. I'm starting to think I'm just not cut out for this."

I asked him, "What do you think is going wrong?"

"Well, I go through the motions. I knock, I smile, I show them the product,but they just don't seem to care," he said, his voice tinged with defeat. "I'm not sure if it's me, or if they just don't see the value."

It was clear to me right away that Michael was missing something fundamental. He was treating the customer like a target—someone to close, someone to convince. But selling isn't about convincing people; it's about helping them realize that they need what you have to offer. It's about creating a connection, a trust, and showing them how your productis the answer to their needs. And that's where Michael had lost his way.

THE TURNING POINT

That night, Michael sat in his car after another unsuccessful day of knocking doors. He sat there in silence, reflecting. He thought about his conversations with potential customers, about the way he pitched the product, and about how he had been focusing so much on the product itself, rather than on the person he was trying to sell to.

It was then that he had a breakthrough moment.

He realized that he had been approaching selling all wrong. He wasn't selling to the person standing in front of him; he was selling to a script, toa set of features, to a concept of "what people want." He was pushing. And in sales, pushing never works.

The next day, Michael decided to take a completely different approach. Instead of focusing on the product, he would focus on the person—their needs, their struggles, their goals. He wasn't going to talk about the vacuum cleaner right away. He was going to start by listening.

So, the next morning, Michael knocked on his first door with a new mindset. Instead of diving straight into his sales pitch, he simply smiled and asked, "What's the hardest part about keeping your house clean?"

The woman who opened the door looked at him for a moment, taken aback. It wasn't the typical "Hi, I'm selling vacuums" introduction. But she soon found herself talking about her kids, her pets, and the endless struggle of keeping up with the mess in her home. Michael listened. He didn't interrupt. He didn't try to sell. He just listened, empathizing withher challenges.

And then, when the time was right, he simply asked, "What if there was a way to make cleaning easier? What if there was a vacuum that could handle pet hair, that could get deep into your carpets, and give you more time to spend with your family?"

The woman paused, considering. She hadn't been looking for a vacuum cleaner that day. But suddenly, she realized that she needed one. Her frustration had a solution, and Michael had helped her uncover that solution. It wasn't about the product— it was about her. It was about her home, her time, and her needs.

In that moment, Michael made the sale—not because he had pushed, but because he had helped the customer realize that his product was the answerto her problem.

IT'S ABOUT BUILDING RELATIONSHIPS, NOT CLOSING DEALS

Michael's experience was a pivotal lesson in the art of selling. He learned that selling isn't about pushing a product on someone; it's about helping them realize that your product is exactly what they've been looking for. It's about creating a relationship of trust, and solving a problem that truly matters to them. Sales, in its purest form, is an extension of that relationship. It's about offering value, and letting the customer come to the conclusion that your offer is the best fit for their needs.

So, how can you become a master at this art of selling? Let's break it down.

STEP 1: UNDERSTAND YOUR CUSTOMER'S NEEDS

Selling begins long before you ever make contact with a potential customer. The foundation of great sales is understanding who your customer is and what they truly need. This isn't just about demographics or market research—it's about understanding their struggles, their pain points, their goals, and what keeps them up at night.

Imagine you're a consultant offering a software product designed to help small businesses track inventory. Your first step isn't to talk about features or functions. Instead, ask yourself: What are the small business owners struggling with? Maybe they're overwhelmed by disorganized inventory systems, or perhaps they're losing sales because they can't track their stock levels in real-time. Your job is to identify that need.

Once you've identified the need, you can position your product as the solution. But here's the key: you must truly understand the problem your customer is facing, because if you don't, you'll never be able to convince them that your solution is the right one.

STEP 2: BUILD TRUST THROUGH LISTENING

When Michael first started his journey into sales, he didn't realize that listening was as important—if not more important—than talking. Yet, when you listen attentively to your customers, you create a bond that is built on understanding and empathy.

Instead of focusing on what you want to say next, focus on what your customer is saying. Listen to their concerns. Ask follow-up questions that show you're genuinely interested in their situation. The more you listen, the more you'll be able to tailor your pitch to their specific needs. When customers feel heard, they feel valued, and they are more likely to trust you with their business.

STEP 3: FOCUS ON BENEFITS, NOT FEATURES

Once you've built that trust through listening, the next step is to position your product or service as the solution to their problem. But here's the thing: don't talk about the features. People don't buy features—they buy benefits. They don't care about how many gigabytes your software offers; they care about how it will save them time or make their business more efficient.

Take a moment to step into your customer's shoes. If you're selling a vacuum cleaner, don't talk about the motor power or the filtration system right away. Talk about how it will save them time. Talk about how it will give them a cleaner home, with less effort. Talk about how it will reduce the stress of constant cleaning. Once they understand how your product will benefit them, then you can go into the details.

STEP 4: SHOW SOCIAL PROOF AND STORIES

One of the most powerful ways to build credibility and close a sale is to share stories. People connect with stories. They don't connect with statistics. When you share a story of how your product or service has helped someone else, you make it tangible, real, and relatable.

Share testimonials from other customers who were in similar situations. Tell stories about how your product made a difference in people's lives. Show them that they are not alone in their struggles and that other people have already found success with your solution.

STEP 5: CLOSE WITH CONFIDENCE—BUT DON'T PUSH

Closing the sale is often the hardest part for many salespeople. They hesitate because they don't want to be pushy. But closing doesn't have to feel like a battle. If you've done your job right—if you've built trust, understood your customer's needs, and presented a solution that works—closing should be a natural step.

The key to closing with confidence is to give the customer a reason to act now. Maybe there's a limited-time offer, or maybe their pain point is urgent. But whatever the reason, make sure the urgency comes from them, not from you.

CONCLUSION

At the core of successful selling lies a fundamental truth: it is never about simply convincing people to buy something they don't need. In fact, true selling is far more nuanced and meaningful. It's about serving others—recognizing their needs, understanding their pain points, and offering a solution that will truly make a positive difference in their lives. The essence of selling, when approached with authenticity and integrity, is rooted in providing value and improving the circumstances of those you serve.

Selling, at its heart, is not a mere transactional act; it is an act of service, a chance to offer something that can genuinely enhance someone's life. This mindset shifts the focus from the seller's agenda to the customer's needs. It's about understanding that every person who walks into your space, whether physical or virtual, comes with a unique set of challenges or desires. Your product or service, in its best form, should align with those challenges, offering solutions that elevate their situation and meet theirneeds.

Take Michael, for example—a person who came to understand this philosophy through firsthand experience. When Michael entered the sales world, he initially approached it with the typical mindset of many: the goalwas simply to close deals, push products, and make numbers. However,he quickly realized that this approach, driven by pressure and tactics, was not sustainable. Instead, he discovered that true success in sales came when he shifted his focus. Rather than trying to push a product or service onto someone, he began to approach every conversation with the mindset of helping.

By taking the time to listen—truly listen—to the people he served, Michael built deeper, more meaningful relationships. He began to view each interaction not as a transaction but as an opportunity to understand the problems, aspirations, and challenges of the person on the other side. In doing so, he was able to offer solutions that were tailored specifically to the needs and desires of his customers.

When you approach selling with this mindset, the sales process transforms. It's no longer about trying to force someone into a decision or manipulate their emotions. Instead, it becomes a conversation rooted in empathy, trust, and genuine care for the customer's well-being. Listening is key here—not just hearing words but understanding the underlying feelings, concerns, and motivations that drive a person's decisions. By connecting with the customer on a deeper level, you're able to offer real, impactfulsolutions that align with their true needs.

Trust is the cornerstone of any meaningful relationship, and it's no different in sales. When you consistently demonstrate that you are more interested in the customer's success than in making a sale, trust naturally follows. This trust builds the foundation for long-term relationships, where customers feel valued and understood rather than just like another sale on the books. When customers trust you, they not only buy from you— they become loyal, returning customers who view your product or service as anessential part of their lives.

Building value also plays a significant role in this equation. It's not justabout offering a product or service; it's about communicating the valuethat product or service brings to the customer. A successful salesperson doesn't simply showcase features; they highlight how those features translate into real-world benefits. Whether it's saving time, reducing stress, improving efficiency, or making life easier, the focus should alwaysbe on how the customer's life will improve as a result of the product orservice being offered.

The more you offer solutions and build value, the more natural the sales process becomes. You're no longer pushing a product; you're facilitating a transformation—helping customers solve their problems and improve their situations. And, as Michael learned, when you approach selling from a service-oriented perspective, the sales will often come naturally. When people feel heard, respected, and valued, they are more likely to invest in what you are offering.

Moreover, selling in this way can also be incredibly fulfilling. It's not about chasing quotas or rushing through transactions. Instead, it's about making a genuine impact, creating positive change, and knowing yourproduct or service is making a real difference in someone's life. The success you experience in sales will not be measured merely by the numbers you hit, but by the difference you make in your customers' lives—helping them find solutions, meet their needs, and achieve their goals.

CHAPTER 10: HOW TO COMMUNICATE RIGHT WITHCUSTOMERS

Effective communication lies at the heart of every successful business, serving as the lifeblood that sustains relationships, drives growth, and establishes a lasting presence in the marketplace. It's not merely the transactional exchange of words, ideas, or information—rather, it's an intricate and dynamic process that creates deep connections, fosters mutual understanding, and cultivates trust. In a world where businesses are constantly vying for attention in an increasingly competitive and crowded marketplace, the ability to communicate effectively with customers becomes more than just a valuable skill; it becomes a cornerstone of business success.

In today's rapidly evolving commercial landscape, customers are faced with a constant bombardment of messages from countless businesses, each vying for a slice of their attention. Whether you're selling a product, offering a service, or simply engaging in an ongoing relationship with yourclients, the way you communicate with them can make or break the future of your business. Effective customer communication isn't just about providing information; it's about creating an experience, establishing rapport, and cultivating trust that will encourage customers to return and recommend your business to others. Without a clear and purposeful communication strategy, a business is at risk of losing not only its competitive edge but also its customer base, as they will likely seek more engaging, responsive, and personalized experiences elsewhere.

At its essence, communication with customers goes far beyond simply "talking to" them. Rather, it is about creating meaningful, two-way interactions that allow businesses to connect with their customers in a way that feels personal, thoughtful, and considerate. It's about understanding customer needs and concerns on a deeper level, and responding in a way that not only solves problems but also makes customers feel heard, valued, and respected. When communication is handled well, it has the power to transform a business from a faceless, impersonal entity into a brand that customers feel emotionally connected to—a brand that they trust and advocate for.

However, communication is a double-edged sword. When it falters or failsto meet the expectations of customers, it can lead to frustration, confusion, and resentment. Customers may feel alienated or disregarded, which can result in negative word-of-mouth, lost opportunities, and dwindling sales. In many cases, poor communication can cause irreparable damage to a brand's reputation, as customers are quick to share their bad experiences, particularly in today's world of social media and online reviews. Therefore, understanding the art of effective communication is not just a matter of improving the quality of your customer interactions—it is essential to the long-term viability of your business.

Let's take a deeper look at the critical principles that underpin effectivecommunication with customers, exploring both the theoretical foundationsand practical applications that can help elevate your customer interactions from the mundane to the extraordinary. Through the lens of both tried-and- true methods and modern innovations, we will uncover the core elements of customer communication that can set your business apart, build lasting loyalty, and turn customers into enthusiastic brand ambassadors.

First and foremost, the foundation of effective communication is active listening. Far too often, businesses make the mistake of thinking that communication is a one-way street, where they simply "tell" customers what they think they need to hear. However, effective communication with customers requires more than just broadcasting your message—it requires tuning in to their needs, wants, and pain points. Listening attentively allows you to fully understand the issues at hand and respond in a way that is relevant, empathetic, and solution-oriented. Active listening fosters a sense of respect and consideration, signaling to customers that their opinions and experiences matter to you. This not only helps resolve immediate concerns but also builds a relationship of trust that can lead to greater satisfaction and repeat business.

Equally important is the ability to communicate clearly and concisely. In a world where customers are constantly bombarded with information, businesses must ensure that their messages are both easy to understand and engaging. Whether you're explaining a product feature, answering a question, or addressing a complaint, clarity is key. Avoid jargon or overly technical language that could confuse or alienate your customers. Instead, use simple, straightforward language that communicates your message in a way that is accessible to everyone. Clear communication also involves setting appropriate expectations—if there are delays, limitations, or issues that might affect a customer's experience, it's important to communicate those proactively rather than leaving them to discover problems on their own.

Furthermore, personalization is an essential aspect of effective communication. Today's customers expect businesses to understand their individual preferences and needs. They don't just want to be another faceless transaction—they want to feel like they matter. Personalizing your communication, whether through tailored emails, personalized recommendations, or customer-specific offers, can go a long way in making customers feel valued and understood. Personalization demonstrates that you see them as more than just a number or a sale—itshows that you care about their unique experience and are invested in meeting their specific needs.

Another critical aspect of effective customer communication is responsiveness. In today's fast-paced, always-connected world, customers expect timely responses to their inquiries, concerns, and feedback. Delays in communication can create frustration and erode trust, particularly when customers feel that their concerns are not being taken seriously. Whether through email, phone calls, social media, or live chat, businesses must prioritize responding promptly and efficiently. Even if you don't have an immediate solution, acknowledging the customer's concern and assuring them that you're working on it goes a long way in building confidence and maintaining a positive relationship.

Moreover, businesses must be consistent in their communication across all channels. Whether a customer interacts with you in-store, on your website, via email, or on social media, the experience should be seamless and consistent. Inconsistent messaging can lead to confusion and a lack of trust, as customers might wonder whether they're dealing with different facets of your business or the same entity. Consistency also extends to the tone and voice of your communication. Whether it's friendly and casual or formal and professional, your communication should align with your brand's identity and reflect the values you want to project.

Real-world examples of businesses that excel in customer communication can provide valuable insights into how these principles are put into action. Take, for instance, companies like Zappos, known for their exceptional customer service. Zappos has built a reputation for going above and beyond to listen to and understand their customers, responding to queries with warmth, empathy, and efficiency. They have created a customer-centric culture where communication isn't just about making a sale—it's about creating a positive and lasting impression that will keep customers coming back for more.

In contrast, many businesses have experienced the fallout from poor communication. Companies that neglect to address customer concerns ina timely manner or fail to listen to feedback risk damaging their reputationand losing business. One only needs to look at the numerous examples of online customer complaints and negative reviews to see the impact that inadequate communication can have on a brand's image.

The art of effective customer communication isn't something that can be mastered overnight—it requires ongoing effort, reflection, and adaptation. As technology continues to evolve, so too do customer expectations. New tools and platforms emerge that provide businesses with innovative ways to engage with their audience, and these must be embraced as part of an integrated communication strategy.

From chatbots to AI-driven customer service, businesses must stay ahead of the curve, leveraging new technologies to enhance their customer communication while maintaining the human touch that makes those interactions truly meaningful.

THE POWER OF COMMUNICATION IN CUSTOMER SERVICE

Before we dive into the details of how to communicate right with customers, it's important to understand why communication is so powerful. Communication shapes every interaction a customer has with your business. It sets the tone, builds the atmosphere, and influences thecustomer's perception of your brand.

Communication is what allows businesses to:

1.   **Build Trust:** Trust is the foundation of every customer relationship. When you communicate effectively, you show that you care about your customer's needs and are dedicated to providing value. Customers trust brands that are transparent, clear,and consistent in their messaging.

2.   **Foster Loyalty:** Loyal customers are the backbone of a successful business. Good communication helps create positive experiences that make customers feel valued and appreciated. This leads to repeat business and long-term customer relationships.

3.   **Resolve Problems:** No business is perfect. There will inevitably be times when customers face issues with your product or service. Effective communication is essential in these moments, as it helps you resolve problems swiftly and satisfactorily.

4.   **Enhance Customer Experience:** The overall

customer experience depends on how well you communicate at every touchpoint. Whether it's in person, over the phone, or through email, every interaction is an opportunity to enhance the customer's experience and leave a positive impression.

THE ART OF LISTENING

Communication isn't just about speaking; it's also about listening. In fact, listening is the most important skill you can develop when communicating with customers. Active listening goes beyond simply hearing the words your customer is saying—it involves understanding their message and recognizing their emotional needs.

One of the biggest mistakes businesses make is assuming they already know what the customer wants or needs. It's easy to fall into the trap ofthinking that you have all the answers, but the reality is, your customers are experts on their own lives, needs, and problems. By truly listening, you open the door to better understanding their situation and providing the right solution.

Let's consider the following example:

THE CASE OF THE FRUSTRATED CUSTOMER

Imagine a customer walks into your store visibly upset. She walks up to the counter and starts speaking about a product she purchased that didn't meet her expectations. If you immediately jump in with an explanation ora solution, you may miss out on the most important part of the conversation: her feelings.

A common mistake is to try to fix the problem before fully understanding the customer's perspective. A customer may feel dismissed or unheard if they don't feel like you've listened to their frustrations. Instead, try saying something like, "I'm really sorry you're feeling frustrated. I'd love to understand more about what happened." By starting with empathy and showing that you care, you allow the customer to open up and share their full experience.

KEY STRATEGIES FOR ACTIVE LISTENING

Give your full attention: In today's fast-paced world, distractions are everywhere. When communicating with a customer, it's essential to put aside everything else and focus on them. Whether it's in person, on the phone, or over chat, make sure you're fully present and not multitasking.

- **Show empathy:** Active listening goes hand-in-hand with empathy. Let the customer know that you understand their feelings. Simple phrases like, "I can understand how frustrating that must be" or "I can see why that would be upsetting" can go a long way in building rapport.

- **Ask open-ended questions:** To fully understand your customer's needs, ask questions that encourage them to elaborate. Instead of asking, "Is everything okay with your product?" try, "Can you tell me more about what's going on with the product?" Open-ended questions help gather important details and show that you're interested in understanding the whole situation.

- **Restate or paraphrase:** When you restate what the customer has said, it shows that you are listening attentively. It also helps to ensure you've understood the issue correctly. For example, "So, what I'm hearing is that the product didn't meet your expectations because it wasn't as described in the ad. Is that right?"

EMPATHY

Once you've actively listened, the next step is empathy. Empathy is the ability to understand and share the feelings of another person. When you empathize with a customer, you show them that their experience matters to you. It's about acknowledging their emotions and validating their feelings.

Empathy can be particularly powerful when dealing with customer complaints. Think about a time you've dealt with an issue—whether it was a late delivery, a defective product, or a misunderstood expectation. The frustration you feel in those moments is real, and your customers feel it too. Responding with empathy shows that you care about their experience and are committed to resolving the issue.

Consider the story of Sarah, who called a tech support center for help with her laptop. She had been having issues for days, and her patience was running thin. When she explained her problem to the support representative, the first thing he said was, "I'm really sorry to hear you're having trouble with your laptop. That must be frustrating. Let's see how we can get this sorted out for you."

By acknowledging Sarah's frustration, the representative immediately put her at ease. She felt heard, and as a result, she was more receptive to the help he provided. Empathy is not just a nice-to-have; it's a must-have for every customer interaction.

THE KEY ELEMENTS OF EMPATHY IN COMMUNICATION

- **Acknowledge their feelings:** When a customer expresses frustration or disappointment, acknowledge it. Saying things like, "I completely understand your frustration" or "I know this situation must be difficult for you" validates their emotions and shows that you're not just focused on solving the issue, but on how they're feeling.

- **Be patient:** Sometimes, customers just need someone to listen to them vent. Don't interrupt or rush them; let them express themselves fully. Giving customers the time and space to articulate their concerns can defuse tension and create a stronger bond.

- **Be sincere:** Customers can tell when empathy is genuine versus when it's just a formality. Avoid using scripted lines or empty phrases. Instead, speak from the heart, and be authentic in your response.

THE IMPORTANCE OF TONE AND LANGUAGE

The way you communicate with your customers also depends on your tone and language. Tone is a subtle yet powerful form of communication. The same words can have very different meanings depending on how they're said. A warm, friendly tone can make a customer feel valued, while a cold, distant tone can create distance.

Let's go back to Lily and Grace from earlier. When Lily first handed Grace the soup, she didn't use any tone to make the interaction feel warm or personal. It was simply business as usual. However, when she later approached Grace with a friendlier, genuine tone—asking about her day and checking on the soup—it made all the difference.

THE IMPACT OF TONE ON CUSTOMER EXPERIENCE

- **Positive tone:** A positive, friendly tone sets the stage for a pleasant interaction. It encourages customers to engage with you and can turn a negative situation into a positive one. In customer service, positivity is contagious.
- **Calm and composed:** In situations where a customer is angry or upset, a calm and composed tone can help de-escalate the situation. When you speak in a calm, reassuring voice, it often helps the customer feel more in control of the conversation.
- **Confident and knowledgeable:** Customers want to know that you know what you're talking about. Speaking confidently about your product or service helps instill trust. However, make sure your confidence doesn't come across as arrogance. Always be willing to admit when you don't know something, but assure the customer that you will find the answer.

CLARITY AND CONCISENESS

Clear communication is essential when interacting with customers. Customers don't have time for long-winded explanations or complicated jargon. They want to understand the solution to their problem quickly and clearly. The best way to achieve this is by being both concise and precise.

While brevity is important, clarity should never be sacrificed for the sake of speed. Don't confuse conciseness with being vague. Being clear means saying exactly what needs to be said, without over-explaining or going off-topic. Avoid jargon or technical terms unless your customer is familiar with them.

For example, if a customer calls to inquire about a return policy, don't say, "Our return policy is as per the terms and conditions available on our website, but if you want to read it, you can go there and find the section on returns." Instead, you could say, "Our return policy allows for returns within 30 days of purchase, provided the product is in unused condition. Would you like me to walk you through the process?"

This approach is clear, concise, and informative. It tells the customer exactly what they need to know, without confusion.

DELIVERING ON YOUR PROMISES

The final, and perhaps most important, aspect of communication is follow through. Customers remember what you say, and they expect you to act on it. Whether it's a promise to resolve an issue, a guarantee to deliver on time, or an offer to follow up, your ability to follow through on your commitments is crucial.

When you make a promise to a customer—whether it's a solution to a problem, a time frame for delivery, or a follow-up call—make sure you deliver. If you say you'll call back in 24 hours, do it. If you promise to issue a refund, do it promptly. Customers value consistency and reliability, and they will remember your follow-through long after the interaction is over.

CLOSING THOUGHTS

Effective communication is not merely a skill—it's a

profound and multifaceted art that encompasses so much more than the simple exchange of information. At its core, communication is the bridge that connects you to your customers on a deeply human level. It's about more than just understanding what they are saying; it's about comprehending their underlying emotions, needs, and desires, and responding in ways that reflect both empathy and clarity. The true essence of effective communication lies in its ability to foster a sense of connection, trust, and mutual respect, transforming the way customers perceive your brand and your service.

When communication is executed with precision and care, it does far more than just address an immediate concern—it serves as the foundation upon which lasting relationships are built. The ability to communicate effectively can transform a transactional encounter into a meaningful interaction, one that resonates with the customer long after the conversation has ended. This is the power of communication: it allows you to go beyond resolving problems and creates a sense of loyalty and trust that can last for years.

Imagine a scenario where you engage with a customer who is frustrated, perhaps even upset, about a product or service issue. Instead of seeing this interaction as just another task to check off your list, view it as an opportunity—a moment to leave a positive and lasting impact. This is when effective communication becomes truly transformative. By taking the time to listen carefully to the customer's concerns, you show that their voice matters, and that you value their perspective. Empathy plays a key role here: by understanding not only what the customer is saying but also how they feel, you are able to respond in a way that acknowledges their emotions and reassures them that you are committed to solving their issue.

But communication doesn't stop at merely listening and empathizing. It's equally important to respond clearly and effectively. A clear, concise, and thoughtful response not only demonstrates that you understand the issue but also that you are capable of addressing it. It's about providing solutions in a way that is both easy for the customer to understand and actionable. This clarity is essential to avoid any further frustration or confusion, and it builds confidence in your ability to meet their needs.

Moreover, the way you follow through on promises plays a critical role in shaping the customer's perception of your communication and service. Promises that are made but not kept can quickly erode trust, while those that are fulfilled reinforce your commitment to the customer's satisfaction. By following through on your commitments, you show the customer that they can rely on you, not just for a quick resolution, but for consistent, dependable service.

Every interaction with a customer—whether it involves answering a simple question or addressing a more complex complaint—presents an invaluable opportunity to build a relationship. These moments, often fleeting, have the potential to transform a one-time customer into a loyal advocate, someone who will return time and again and recommend your business to others. But to achieve this, it requires intentional and thoughtful communication in every step of the process.

Think of the vast number of daily interactions that make up your customer service efforts. Each one is an opportunity not just to solve problems but to create lasting impressions. With each interaction, you have the power to reshape the customer's experience, turning frustration into satisfaction, indifference into loyalty, and hesitation into advocacy. This ability is the true measure of success in any customer-focused organization.

So, the next time you find yourself in a customer interaction, whether it's over the phone, through email, or face-to-face, remember that communication is not just about what you say— it's about how you say it, how you listen, and how you follow through. Listen deeply, not just to the words but to the emotions behind them. Empathize sincerely, showing that you understand their perspective. Speak clearly and directly, ensuring that your message is both heard and understood. And most importantly, always follow through on your promises, because consistency and dependability are the cornerstones of trust.

Through the power of effective communication, every single customer interaction becomes an opportunity for success—an opportunity to build rapport, to nurture relationships, and to lay the groundwork for future loyalty. Whether your customer is in need of assistance or simply seeking information, the way you engage with them can turn a mundane transaction into an extraordinary experience. This is the true art of communication: not just solving problems, but forging connections that last a lifetime.

CHAPTER 11: KNOW YOUR PRODUCT FIRST, MORE THANYOUR CUSTOMER

There's a secret in the world of sales, customer service, and business success—a secret that most people don't understand until it's too late. It's not about the customer, the market, or even the competition. The secret to being truly successful is knowing your product inside and out. Not justknowing the basic features, but understanding the soul of the product, its purpose, its limitations, its strengths, and its value in a customer's life. The truth is, you can't effectively serve your customer if you don't fully understand what you're offering. You have to know your product betterthan anyone else, even better than the customer themselves.

This concept became crystal clear to me during a pivotal moment early in my career, one I'll never forget. I had just started working in sales at a techcompany that specialized in smart home devices—cutting-edge products that promised to revolutionize the way people interacted with their homes. We sold everything from smart thermostats to security cameras, smart locks, and voice-activated assistants. It was an exciting industry, filled with new and innovative technology that promised to make lives easier, safer, and more connected.

Like most young professionals, I was eager to prove myself. I had big dreams, high aspirations, and an abundance of energy. I was the kind ofperson who could easily connect with others. I was a people person, naturally friendly, approachable, and confident. I believed that my ability to engage with customers and form strong relationships would be enough to make me a top performer. What I didn't realize, however, was that people don't buy from you because you're friendly. They buy from you because you believe in the product you're selling. They buy because you know the product so well that they trust your judgment and expertise.

But at the time, I didn't know the products I was selling nearly as well asI should have. Sure, I knew the basics. I could tell a customer that our smart thermostat adjusted the temperature based on their preferences and saved energy. But when it came to answering detailed questions about integration with other systems, battery life, or even the technical specifications, I faltered. I could connect with people, but I couldn't confidently answer their more technical questions. I would stumble over phrases like, "I'm not entirely sure, but let me check on that for you," or"I think it might work with your system, but I can't be sure."

One particular incident stands out in my memory—an experience that would fundamentally change the way I approached sales and customer service. It was a Wednesday afternoon, and I had a scheduled meeting with Sarah, a potential customer who was considering buying a home security system. Sarah was a tech-savvy woman, someone who had done her research. She wasn't easily impressed, and she didn't want to be sold to.She wanted answers.

I began the conversation confidently, explaining how our security system worked and highlighting its key features. But then she asked me a questionI wasn't prepared for: "Does this system integrate with my existing home automation setup?" I had no idea. I had never asked that question myself, and I certainly hadn't thought to look into how our system worked with other devices. My heart sank. I realized, in that moment, that I was selling something I didn't truly understand. I didn't know enough about the product to help Sarah make an informed decision, and I certainly didn't know enough to earn her trust. I muttered something about checking and promised I'd get back to her, but I knew that the damage had already been done. She left, and I never heard from her again.

That experience was a hard pill to swallow, but it taught me one of the most valuable lessons of my career: You cannot be successful in sales—or in customer service—if you don't understand your product. I had been focused on trying to understand the customer, trying to anticipate their needs and desires, without first fully understanding the product I was offering. I had it all backward.

THE POWER OF PRODUCT KNOWLEDGE

The more I reflected on that moment, the more I realized that product knowledge isn't just a nice-to-have in sales—it's the foundation of everything. Without it, you're merely guessing. You're relying on surface-level information, and that's a dangerous game to play. If you want to build trust, confidence, and long-term relationships with customers, you need to know your product inside and out.

Think about it—when you're shopping for something important, especially a high-investment item like a car, a piece of technology, or a home system, do you want to talk to someone who knows everything about the product? Or do you want to talk to someone who's just there to take your order, with no real expertise? It's an easy choice.

Take the example of buying a luxury car. If you walk into a dealership and the salesperson can't confidently explain the engine specs, the safety features, or the technology built into the car, what does that say to you? It says they're not really invested in the product. It says that they don't believe in it, and if they don't believe in it, how could you?

On the other hand, when you walk into a dealership and the salesperson can articulate every detail of the car—the performance, the safety ratings, the history of the brand, and even the little quirks that make it special—that's when you start to trust them. That's when you start to believe in the product. The salesperson becomes a trusted advisor, someone who is genuinely helping you make an informed decision. They're not just selling—they're educating, guiding, and connecting the product to your needs.

That's the power of product knowledge. When you know your product, you become a resource. You're not just there to answer questions—you're there to offer solutions. You're not just offering a product; you're offering a promise. A promise that this product will meet the customer's needs and deliver value. And when a customer believes that, they'll buy from you. They'll trust you.

A RELATIONSHIP BUILT ON TRUST

One of the most important aspects of sales—and customer service in general—is trust. People want to feel that they're being heard, understood, and respected. But more than that, they want to feel that the person they're working with is knowledgeable. They want to know that the person they're talking to understands the product they're selling, and they want to know that the person can help them make the best choice.

In sales, trust isn't built on charm alone. You can't just smile, be friendly, and hope for the best. You have to build trust through competence. You build trust by demonstrating that you know the product. You build trust by answering questions thoroughly and confidently. You build trust by anticipating needs before they arise and offering solutions that genuinely solve problems.

The key to gaining trust isn't just knowing the features of a product—it's about understanding why those features matter to the customer. You need to understand how the product fits into their life, what problem it solves for them, and why it's the right solution. It's about translating the product's specifications into tangible benefits that resonate with the customer.

Take the time to get to know the ins and outs of your product. Learn its history. Understand how it's made, why it was created, and the problems it's designed to solve. By doing this, you're not just learning facts—you're learning its story. And once you know the story of the product, you can tell it to your customers in a way that captivates them. People love stories.

They connect with them. And when your product becomes part of that story, it becomes more than just a transaction—it becomes a relationship.

THE STORY BEHIND THE PRODUCT

Think about some of the most successful brands in the world. Apple didn't just sell phones—they sold an experience. Tesla doesn't just sell cars—they sell a vision for the future. The products are more than just items—they represent something greater. When you know the story behind your product, you can share that story with your customers. You can explain not just what the product is, but why it matters.

This was a lesson I learned during my time at a company that sold eco-friendly home products. The products weren't just reusable bags and bamboo toothbrushes—they were part of a larger movement to reduce waste and protect the environment. Once I understood that, my sales approach changed. I didn't just sell products—I sold a vision. I explained to customers how every small purchase was part of a bigger solution to a global problem. I didn't just talk about the benefits of the products—I talked about the benefits of being part of the solution.

This shift in perspective transformed my sales performance. Customers didn't just buy because they liked the products—they bought because they felt they were making a difference. They felt like they were part of something bigger, something that aligned with their values. And that made them loyal customers, customers who came back again and again.

HOW TO MASTER PRODUCT KNOWLEDGE

So, how do you become an expert in your product? How do you ensure that you're not just skimming the surface, but truly understanding what you're offering? Here are some strategies that I've used over the years to master product knowledge:

- **Be Hands-On:** There's no substitute for

experience. If you're selling a physical product, use it. Test it. Live with it. Understand it from the customer's perspective. The more familiar you are with the product, the better you'll be able to explain it to others.

- **Ask Questions:** Don't just accept surface-level information. Dig deeper. Ask the right questions. Find out what makes the product unique, how it works, and why it's better than the competition.

- **Stay Updated:** Products evolve. Technologies change. Make sure you stay up-to-date with the latest developments, updates, and upgrades. Know when a new version is coming out and what new features will be available.

- **Learn from Others:** Talk to other experts. Listen to customers. Learn from your colleagues and mentors. Share knowledge and exchange insights. This will deepen your understanding and help you see the product from different angles.

- **Read and Research:** Read the product manual. Research the company's history. Look for reviews and feedback from customers. The more information you gather, the better equipped you'll be to answer questions and handle objections.

By following these steps, you'll gain a deeper, more comprehensive understanding of your product—and that knowledge will make you an invaluable resource to your customers.

CONCLUSION

The truth is, knowing your product isn't just about answering questions. It's about building a relationship of trust, confidence, and mutual respect with your customer. It's about understanding the product so deeply that you can anticipate your customer's needs and offer solutions before they even ask.

When you know your product better than anyone else, you become an expert. You become someone your customers trust, someone they turn to when they need advice or guidance. And in business, trust is everything.

So, remember—know your product first. Master it, understand it, and live it. When you do, you'll find that understanding your customer becomes second nature.

CHAPTER 12: HAVE UNDERSTANDING AND CONFIDENCE IN YOUR PRODUCT

There was a small bakery in the heart of a bustling town, nestled between an old bookstore and a quaint café. This bakery wasn't the flashiest, nordid it have the most intricate branding. But it had something far more powerful: deep understanding and unshakable confidence in what it offered. And it all began with one simple thing—bread.

Maria, the owner of the bakery, wasn't just the one who ran the shop. She was the one who kneaded the dough, who carefully selected the flour, whowatched over every batch of bread like it was her own child. For Maria, baking wasn't just a business. It was a calling, a craft she had learned and honed over the years, inherited from her grandmother, and passed down through generations.

But the story I want to tell you isn't just about a small, family-run bakery. It's about the power of knowing your product inside and out, and having the confidence that comes from that knowledge. It's about how understanding your product on a deep, intimate level allows you to overcome challenges, impress skeptics, and ultimately create a product that speaks for itself.

THE ARRIVAL OF THE CRITIC

One crisp autumn morning, as the sun cast its golden light

on the cobblestone streets of the town, a new customer entered the bakery. This wasn't just any customer. This man wasn't there for the sweet smell of freshly baked pastries or the soft allure of warm bread. This man was a food critic—one of the most notorious in the region. His opinions could make or break a restaurant, and his reviews were known to shape public perception for years to come.

Maria had heard whispers about this critic. He was known for his sharp tongue and even sharper pen. People talked about how he could tear apart an entire establishment with a single sentence. Some bakers had even stopped trying to impress him, knowing his standards were impossibly high. But Maria wasn't fazed. She had worked with her hands in the kitchen for decades. She had perfected her recipes, fine-tuned her processes, and built a product that was a reflection of her love for the craft.

Her confidence wasn't based on arrogance or naivety—it was rooted in something much more solid: deep knowledge of her product. She knew her bread, inside and out, and there wasn't a question about it that would throw her off course.

As the critic approached the counter, Maria smiled warmly. She didn't ask him if he was there for a review or whether he was going to write about her bakery. She didn't need to. She knew that when people tasted her bread, they experienced it for what it was. It wasn't about the bells and whistles of the bakery; it was about the quality of the product.

"Good morning! How can I help you today?" Maria asked, her tone friendly but unwavering.

The critic looked around the shop with a discerning eye. His gaze was sharp, not missing a detail. Maria could feel the weight of his scrutiny, but she didn't flinch. She had been through this countless times before with regular customers and occasional foodies, and she knew that the best way to respond to such a challenge was with absolute confidence in her product.

"I've heard a lot about your bread," the critic said, his voice cool and measured. "I'm here to try it for myself."

Maria nodded, her expression unchanged. She knew the bread he had come for—the sourdough. It was the one that had won awards, the one that people lined up for every morning, the one that had been crafted with such precision and care that it was almost sacred. She reached for a loaf and placed it gently on the counter.

"The sourdough," Maria said. "It's our signature bread. We start with a natural starter that's been passed down for generations. We allow it to ferment for a full 12 hours before we bake it. The longer fermentation gives it its signature tang and chewy texture. It's made with the best organic flour, sourced from local farms that we know personally."

The critic examined the loaf, turning it over in his hands as if he were weighing it, inspecting its every curve, every crack. "It's a beautiful loaf," he said, his tone skeptical but not dismissive. "But how do you know it will turn out this way every time? What happens if the fermentation doesn't go as planned?"

Maria smiled, as if the question were one she had answered a thousand times before. "The bread tells me when it's ready. The fermentation process is long, yes, but that's what makes it so reliable. Over time, I've learned to listen to it. I know when the starter is at its peak. I can tell by the smell, the bubbles, the texture of the dough. It's a relationship—one that's built on understanding."

The critic raised an eyebrow. He had never heard anyone speak about baking in such personal terms. He had spoken with many chefs and bakers in his time, but Maria's confidence, her absolute trust in her product, was something else entirely.

"So, it's all about experience?" he asked, his interest piqued.

Maria nodded. "Exactly. Experience, patience, and understanding. When you know your product that well, you don't have to guess. You don't have to hope for a good result. You know it's going to turn out exactly as you intend."

The critic nodded slowly, as if he were processing her words. He wasn't a man easily swayed, but he had to admit—there was something about Maria's approach that made sense. It wasn't about cutting corners or rushing the process; it was about mastery. It was about being so attuned to your craft that you couldn't help but create excellence.

THE HEART OF CONFIDENCE

As the critic took his first bite of the sourdough, there was a moment of silence. Maria stood behind the counter, watching him closely. She wasn't nervous—she had nothing to prove. She had confidence that her bread would speak for itself.

He chewed slowly, his expression unreadable. Then, after what felt like an eternity, he finally spoke. "This... this is incredible. The texture is perfect. It's chewy, with just the right amount of tang. But what really stands out is the depth of flavor. I've never had sourdough quite like this before."

Maria smiled, but her smile wasn't the one of someone who had just won a compliment. It was the smile of someone who had known this moment would come. "Thank you," she said simply. "It's the product of a lot of time and care. I'm glad you like it."

The critic leaned back, taking in the entire bakery. "I can see it now. It's not just the bread. It's everything about this place. The care you put into every batch, the time you take to get it right. It's all about understanding your craft and trusting in the process. You're not just selling bread—you're selling something real."

Maria nodded, her confidence growing with every word the critic said. She wasn't selling bread. She was sharing her life's work. She wasn't just offering a product; she was offering her passion, her experience, her deep understanding of the craft.

As the critic left, he didn't just leave with a loaf of sourdough. He left with a story—one that he would share with his readers, one that would inspire others to approach their work with the same level of understanding and confidence.

THE IMPORTANCE OF DEEP PRODUCT KNOWLEDGE

The story of Maria and her bakery teaches us several important lessons. The first, and perhaps the most significant, is the power of deep understanding. When you know your product inside and out, you are not just a seller; you become an expert. An expert doesn't just know the features of their product—they know the history behind it, the process that goes into creating it, and the impact it has on people's lives.

For Maria, the bread was more than just a recipe. It was a legacy. It was the culmination of years of learning, testing, refining, and adapting. She had invested time and energy into understanding every aspect of the baking process—from the choice of ingredients to the timing of fermentation to the specific heat of the oven. This knowledge didn't just make her good at what she did; it made her confident. She knew that no matter what challenges arose, she had the knowledge to overcome them.

When you have this level of understanding, it doesn't just benefit you—it benefits your customers, too. They can tell when you're confident in what you're offering. Confidence is contagious, and when your customers see that you genuinely believe in your product, they are more likely to believe in it, too.

CONFIDENCE WITHOUT ARROGANCE

It's essential to understand that Maria's confidence was not the kind of overt, boastful arrogance that often masks insecurity or the desire to put others down. She did not approach her conversations or interactions with a sense of superiority, nor did she speak as if she had all the answers to

life's questions. There was no sense of puffed-up pride in her demeanor. Instead, her confidence was built on something far more substantial—on the foundation of her deep knowledge and years of hands-on experience. It was a quiet, almost understated confidence—a confidence that came not from claiming perfection, but from having honed her skills through countless hours of practice, learning from both her successes and her mistakes, and cultivating a genuine, profound respect for the work she did and the craft she mastered.

This was the kind of confidence that didn't need to shout to be noticed. It wasn't loud or brash; it didn't seek validation through external praise or applause. It was the kind of confidence that spoke volumes simply by being present. Maria understood, perhaps more than most, that true confidence does not arise from the desire to be better than others, nor does it involve diminishing others to elevate oneself. Rather, it stems from a deep-rooted belief in one's own abilities, in one's value, and in the quiet assurance that your competence speaks for itself. It's the sort of confidence that is grounded in the authenticity of your own journey, built upon years of practice, trial, and error, and ultimately, the lessons you've learned along the way.

True confidence is never about boasting, belittling others, or elevating oneself through comparison. It's never about seeking validation or approval from the outside world in a way that diminishes the worth of others. On the contrary, it's about recognizing and owning your value—without hesitation or apology—and being able to communicate that value to others in a way that is both genuine and humble. It's about walking into a room, not with a sense of entitlement, but with the quiet knowledge that you belong because of your ability, your character, and the work you've put in. It's about being able to stand firm in your convictions, knowing your actions and words reflect a deep and authentic understanding of what you bring to the table, without needing to constantly prove it to others.

When you possess this level of self-assurance, you don't

need to tell people how good you are or boast about your accomplishments. You don't need to constantly remind others of your worth. Instead, your confidence becomes apparent in the way you carry yourself, in how you respond to questions, and in the way you share your thoughts and experiences. It's the kind of confidence that is evident when you answer a question without hesitation, when you offer your advice or expertise with a calm assurance, and when you share your story with the understanding that it is yours to tell, free from the fear of judgment or criticism. You are not concerned with the opinions of others because your confidence is rooted in your own understanding of who you are and what you know.

This kind of deep-rooted confidence doesn't need to be loud or forceful. It doesn't need to rely on external accolades or the need to prove yourself to others. When you are truly confident, your product—whether that's your work, your service, or the value you provide—speaks for itself. The quality of what you offer becomes the loudest testament to your ability. People will notice the caliber of your work. They'll feel the passion and conviction in your words, and they'll experience firsthand the assurance you have in your service. It's a confidence that is contagious, drawing others in not because you are trying to sell them something, but because they can sense the genuine value in what you offer. When your confidence is rooted in your craft, in your experience, and in the quiet certainty that you know what you are doing, you no longer need to seek approval from others. The results, the impact, and the authenticity of your work will communicate all that needs to be said.

And so, Maria's confidence was not a loud declaration of superiority, but a quiet, compelling force that commanded respect simply through its presence. It was the kind of confidence that comes from knowing yourself deeply, from trusting in the journey that has shaped you, and from understanding that when you've put in the work, your value will be recognized, not because you force it, but because it's undeniable.

CONCLUSION

In the end, the lesson from Maria's bakery is simple, but profound: Understand your product deeply, and have confidence in what you offer.

This is the key to success in any field—whether you're a baker, a business owner, an entrepreneur, or a creator of any kind. Your confidence isn't built on hype or empty promises. It's built on years of dedication, experience, and a true understanding of what you're offering.

When you have this level of understanding, not only will your customers trust you, but they will also respect you. They will become loyal to yourbrand, not because of clever marketing, but because they believe in what you stand for. And just like Maria's bakery, your product will speak foritself.

So, invest the time to understand every detail of what you're offering. Get to know your product as if it were a part of you. Build that confidence—not from bragging, but from the quiet assurance that comes from truly mastering your craft. When you do, you'll find that success isn't just a goal—it's a natural byproduct of understanding and believing in your product.

CHAPTER 13: INFORMATION IS POWER

In today's ever-evolving landscape of business, one principle stands the test of time: information is power. It's a phrase we've heard time and again, but its true significance often goes unnoticed, especially in the day-to-day hustle of running a business. What does it truly mean for information to be powerful? And how does it translate from theory into practice, from a mere concept into a tangible strategy that can shape the trajectory of an entire business?

To answer these questions, I want to take you on a journey into a story that reveals the incredible impact that information can have—not just as a tool for efficiency, but as a transformative force capable of creating lasting relationships, generating trust, and fueling sustainable success.

The story I want to share comes from a small, family-owned café in a quiet corner of the city, "The Green Leaf Café." From the outside, the café looked just like any other establishment—modest décor, a warm, welcoming ambiance, and the rich smell of freshly brewed coffee filling the air. There was nothing spectacular about it at first glance. But as you'll soon see, the secret to its success didn't lie in its physical space or its average menu; it came down to one simple, but incredibly powerful practice: gathering, understanding, and utilizing information.

THE SPARK OF REALIZATION

Sarah, the owner of The Green Leaf Café, had always dreamed of owning a coffee shop. She imagined a place where people would not only come for a cup of coffee but also to connect, to find a sense of community. She envisioned a business that would serve as a gathering point for people, where relationships would be built over a shared love for great coffee and friendly conversations.

However, after a few months of operation, Sarah began to realize that the café, despite its growing popularity, lacked something. It had regular customers, but they didn't seem to have the kind of deep, emotional connection to the place that she had hoped for. They came in, ordered their coffee, sat for a while, and left. There was no conversation that went beyond the small talk. No deep bonds were being formed. No customers felt seen or truly understood.

It was one day when Sarah overheard a conversation between two customers that made her pause. One of them was a regular who had been coming in every morning for several weeks. She ordered the same coffee—a cappuccino, extra foam, with a blueberry muffin on the side. As she placed her order, she glanced at Sarah, smiled, and said, "The usual, please." But Sarah could tell that the smile didn't quite reach her eyes. She wasn't upset, but there was a subtle detachment in her demeanor, as if she were simply going through the motions.

Sarah began to wonder: Why was it that this regular customer, who came in every day, still felt like a stranger? Why did she never seem to open up, even though she was a constant presence in the café?

That was the moment Sarah realized that she had to do more than just servecoffee. If she truly wanted her café to be a place where people felt connected, she needed to do something differently. She needed to know her customers—not just their names or their orders, but who they were, what they liked, what made them happy, what made them sad, and whatthey valued in life. She realized that information was the key to unlocking deeper relationships. But, it wasn't just about gathering any type of information—it had to be the right kind of information, shared with care and purpose.

THE FIRST STEP

Sarah wasn't naive. She knew that people didn't always want to share personal details with strangers, and that simply asking customers about their lives might come across as intrusive or awkward. So, she began by observing—watching how her regulars interacted, noticing what they ordered, how they preferred their coffee, and how they carried themselves. Every detail, no matter how small, became important. For instance, there was Mr. Thompson, the elderly man who would always order a cappuccino with extra foam and sit by the window with a book in hand. He was a regular, but he was also solitary, never engaging in conversation. Yet, there was something about him that made Sarah feel like he was waiting for something more—like he wasn't just there for the coffee, but for something deeper.

As Sarah began to interact more personally with her regulars, she started asking subtle questions—nothing too invasive, just simple things like, "How's your day been so far?" or "What's new with you this week?" Somecustomers responded with casual answers, but others started to open up. It wasn't long before Sarah had learned that Mr. Thompson had recently lost his wife, and that his daily visits to the café were not just about the cappuccino, but about finding some quiet space to reflect on his memories and feel the presence of her absence.

Then there was Maria, a young mother who came in every morning with her toddler in tow. Maria always ordered a black coffee, no sugar, and barely said a word. Sarah eventually learned that Maria had just moved to the city and was struggling to juggle her demanding job with her responsibilities as a mother. Sarah, ever the listener, made a point of remembering these small details. Over time, Maria began to open up more—sharing not just about her challenges as a mother, but also abouther dreams, her frustrations, and her need for community.

It wasn't magic. It wasn't something that happened overnight. But by consistently paying attention to the little things, Sarah was gathering information—information that wasn't just about what people ordered, but about who they were as people. With that information, she was able to serve her customers in a way that went far beyond just handing over a cup of coffee. She was able to anticipate their needs, to understand their moods, and to create an environment that made them feel known.

ANTICIPATION

Once Sarah began gathering this information, something extraordinary happened. She started to anticipate the needs of her customers before they even voiced them. She noticed that Mr. Thompson, for example, would often come in on particularly cold mornings and spend longer than usual sitting by the window, lost in thought. On those days, Sarah would make sure to warm up his cappuccino just a little extra before serving it to him. It wasn't something she had to say out loud; the mere act of anticipating his needs showed him that she understood his preferences and cared about his comfort.

Maria, the young mother, came in each morning looking tired, but with a look of determination on her face. Sarah quickly realized that Maria's mornings were often rushed, and her coffee was something she relied on to fuel her day. Sarah started preparing her coffee just the way Maria liked it, even before Maria made it to the counter. She would greet her with a warm, "How's your little one today?" and hand her a perfectly prepared coffee to go. Over time, Maria began to feel a sense of comfort and familiarity with Sarah's café. She didn't just come for the coffee; she came for the experience—the feeling that someone cared about her, that someone saw her beyond her role as a mother, as an employee, and as a customer.

This practice of anticipation wasn't just about making customers feel good in the moment—it was about building a relationship. It was about making each customer feel like they were more than just a transaction. Every time a customer walked into The Green Leaf Café, they were greeted with more than just a smile. They were greeted with a thoughtful experience, one that was tailored to their needs, their preferences, and even their unspoken desires.

THE POWER OF PERSONALIZED ATTENTION

As Sarah's café continued to grow in popularity, the power of personalized attention became increasingly apparent. Customers didn't just come in for the coffee—they came in because they felt a sense of belonging. The Green Leaf Café had transformed from a typical coffee shop into a community hub, a place where people could connect not only with their favorite drink but with others who shared similar experiences.

One morning, Sarah overheard a conversation between two regulars who had never spoken much before. One of them said, "You know, I've been coming here for months, and Sarah always remembers my name. It's like she knows exactly what I need without me having to say anything." The other customer responded, "It's not just about the coffee. It's the way she makes you feel like you matter. Like you're more than just another customer."

That, in a nutshell, is the power of information. It's not just about knowing someone's preferences—it's about knowing who they are and using that knowledge to create an experience that goes beyond their expectations. Sarah's ability to gather and use information had transformed her café into something far more valuable than just a business—it had turned it into a community.

TRUST AND LOYALTY

As Sarah continued to implement this practice of gathering and using information, she began to see the fruits of her labor. Customers who once felt like faceless individuals walking into a café now felt like part of something larger. They felt known, appreciated, and valued.

What's more, this approach didn't just create satisfaction—it created trust. When customers trust that a business understands them, that business becomes more than just a service provider. It becomes a trusted partner in their daily lives. And when people trust a business, they return. They don't just return—they advocate for the business. Word of mouth spread quickly, and before long, the café was no longer just a neighborhood coffee shop—it was a local institution.

One day, Sarah overheard a conversation that perfectly encapsulated the power of information. Two new customers were sitting at the bar, enjoying their coffee. One said to the other, "You've got to try this place. They remember everything about you. I'm telling you, it's like they really care."

And that's the ripple effect of information. It's not just about improving customer satisfaction in the moment—it's about building trust that leads to loyalty, and ultimately, to advocacy. And that advocacy is invaluable.It creates a network of customers who are not just satisfied—they're emotionally invested. They're not just buyers—they're promoters. They will tell others about the experience, and soon, your business will have an army of loyal supporters who help you grow without spending a penny on advertising.

CONCLUSION

The lesson here is both simple and profound: Information is undeniably power, but its true value is unlocked only when it is approached with intention, care, and purpose. In the fast-paced world we live in today, it's easy to become overwhelmed by the sheer volume of data that we are constantly bombarded with. We can gather endless amounts of information, but simply amassing facts, figures, and statistics will never be enough to create a truly meaningful impact. The true power of information comes from how we choose to use it—not as a passive resource, but as a dynamic tool that can be strategically applied to createlasting, authentic connections.

Imagine information as a raw ingredient—it's what you do with it that determines whether it becomes something of value. It's not just about collecting data for the sake of having it. It's about carefully analyzing that data, interpreting it, and then using it to shape experiences that resonate deeply with your audience. Information becomes potent when it's used to anticipate needs, respond to desires, and craft personalized experiences that leave a lasting impression. When deployed correctly, it becomes the cornerstone of extraordinary customer relationships—relationships that go beyond mere transactions and evolve into genuine emotional connections.

Take the example of Sarah and her café. On the surface, a café might seem like just another place to grab a quick cup of coffee and go about your day. However, Sarah's café transformed into something far more significant. It became a haven—a place where people didn't just stop by to refuel; they felt truly seen, heard, and valued. People came not only for the quality of the coffee but for the feeling of being understood and appreciated. And how did Sarah create this kind of environment? Through the thoughtful, intentional use of information.

Sarah didn't just know her customers as faceless patrons who buy her coffee and left. She took the time to learn their preferences, understand their routines, and pay attention to the subtle cues that revealed what made each person feel special. Whether it was remembering a customer's favorite drink or asking about their family, Sarah's café became a place where people felt like more than just a number. It was a place where their needs were anticipated before they even voiced them. This wasn't a coincidence—it was the result of careful, intentional observation and the thoughtful application of information.

Now, what does this mean for you and your business? It means that if you can master the art of using information with intention and purpose, you'll be able to transform your customer interactions from simple transactions into meaningful, relational experiences. It's about going beyond the basics and tapping into the deeper emotional layer of your customers' needs. When you use information not just to serve, but to truly connect, you buildsomething far more valuable than a one-time sale. You build relationships.

Relationships are the lifeblood of any successful business. In today's world, customers crave more than just a product or service—they want to feel valued and appreciated. They want to know that you see them as individuals, not just as consumers. And relationships, as we all know, are built on trust, loyalty, and consistency. When customers feel understood, when they know that you are listening and responding to their unique needs, they become loyal to your brand. They return time and time again—not because they have to, but because they trust you. They trust that youhave their best interests at heart. This trust is the bedrock of long-term success.

It's easy to get caught up in the numbers—the sales figures, the conversion rates, the customer demographics—but if you focus solely on these metrics, you may miss the bigger picture. True customer loyalty isn't won by offering the lowest price or the quickest transaction. It's won by offering something far more valuable: an experience that feels personal, thoughtful, and authentic. When you treat your customers like people, not transactions, they'll reward you with their loyalty.

So, the next time you find yourself interacting with a customer—whether it's in person, over the phone, or online—remember this: information is power. But it's not enough to simply gather data. You must use it wisely. Use it to understand your customers on a deeper level, to anticipate their needs before they express them, and to create experiences that make them feel valued. When you do this, you'll unlock a world of possibilities. You'll build relationships that go beyond the transactional and pave the way for lasting loyalty and success.

CHAPTER 14: HOW TO KEEP SELLING AND MAKE PROFIT

Selling is far more than just a transaction or closing a single deal. It's a comprehensive, ongoing journey that demands an intricate, systematic approach. At its core, sales is about crafting a sustainable, consistent, and scalable process that allows you to generate revenue over time. It is about much more than hitting a quick target; it's about developing a mechanism that nurtures long-term growth, profitability, and resilience. For many entrepreneurs, the initial thrill of launching a new product or service can quickly fade when the realization sets in: sales don't just happen spontaneously. They require deliberate, persistent effort, strategic adjustments, and an unwavering commitment to innovation.

At the start of a new venture, there is often an overwhelming sense of excitement. You launch your business with dreams of success, imagining that your hard work will quickly translate into sales. But as days turn into weeks and weeks into months, you come to understand that building a successful sales model is far from a simple task. It takes time, planning, testing, and refinement. Sales don't just happen by magic; they require a continuous cycle of effort, learning, and adaptation. Every new day presents a fresh set of challenges, each one demanding a new strategy, a new approach, or a new solution. It is this ongoing process that separates businesses that thrive from those that fail.

Whether you're selling a product for the first time, or

you've been in business for years, this chapter is not just for beginners. It's for anyonewho has experienced the many highs and lows of running a business—those who have felt the weight of fluctuating sales, shifting markets, and tough competition, and are now looking to uncover the secrets to long-term success. It's for those who want to learn how to stay in the game, continue generating sales, and ensure that the business remains profitable for the long haul. The truth is, business success doesn't rely on a one-time win or a burst of enthusiasm. It relies on creating a process that keeps moving forward, even when things get tough.

Now, let's take a moment to imagine a ship sailing across a vast, unpredictable ocean. On calm days, the sea is flat, the sky is clear, and the ship glides smoothly forward with little resistance. The journey feels effortless. However, when the storms roll in, and the waves start crashing against the hull, the ship is tossed around, vulnerable to the ferocity of nature. Without the right preparation and adjustments, the ship could easily capsize and sink. The captain must remain vigilant, adjusting the sails and navigating the ship through turbulent waters to keep it on course.

This metaphor is deeply reflective of the business journey. In calm periods,things may seem easy—sales are flowing, profits are up, and everything feels right. But just like the unpredictable ocean, the market is always changing. Competition increases, consumer preferences shift, and economic factors can change the direction of your business. Without the right tools, mindset, and ability to adapt, your business can easily lose its way. Just as the ship requires constant navigation and adjustments, so too does your business. You cannot afford to sit idle or expect that successwill come automatically.

The key to staying afloat in business lies in resilience, consistency, and innovation. Resilience allows you to weather the storms, consistency ensures that your sales process remains strong even during slow periods, and innovation helps you to adjust and stay relevant. These principles are the foundation of a sustainable sales strategy, and they will guide you through the ups and downs of business.

Consider the story of Morning Bliss, a small, family-owned coffee shop that found its footing during challenging times. When it first opened, Morning Bliss had the same hopes and dreams as many other businesses: a steady stream of customers, thriving sales, and a strong community presence. But like many small businesses, the shop faced unforeseen challenges. The initial novelty wore off, and customer traffic began to dwindle. The owners quickly realized that sales could not be sustained on hope and goodwill alone—they needed to rethink their approach.

Instead of getting discouraged, the owners took action. They realized that in order to survive, they needed to stay flexible and continually adapt. They began by enhancing their product offerings, introducing seasonal drinks, and experimenting with new flavors that appealed to their customers' tastes. But it wasn't just about the products; they also focused on the customer experience. Morning Bliss became more than just a coffee shop—it became a community hub. They hosted local events, offered loyalty programs, and engaged with their customers through social media.

As the coffee shop adjusted its offerings and engagement strategies, it became clear that success was not about short bursts of excitement. Rather, it was about long-term commitment, patience, and consistent effort. Over time, the shop built a loyal customer base, increased its sales, and turned the business around. This transformation didn't happen overnight. It was the result of months of trial and error, strategic adjustments, and a deep commitment to staying the course.

The story of Morning Bliss serves as a powerful reminder that business success is not a sprint—it's a marathon. In a world that often celebrates overnight success stories, it's important to remember that behind every successful business is a journey of perseverance, learning, and adaptation. Success is not built on fleeting moments of excitement, but on a sustained, deliberate effort to improve and innovate.

In the world of sales, the process is everything. A business cannot rely on one-off sales or occasional wins. The true power lies in creating a sales system that is not only effective but also scalable. This means having the foresight to understand what works and continuously refining and optimizing the process. It involves using data and insights to track performance, identifying opportunities for improvement, and being open to change.

Moreover, sales strategies need to evolve over time. The market changes, customer needs shift, and technology advances. A strategy that works today may not work tomorrow. Just as a ship captain must continually adjust the sails to navigate through different conditions, business owners must be proactive in evolving their sales strategies to meet the ever- changing demands of the market.

Sales is not a one-time achievement; it's a continuous cycle of growth, learning, and adaptation. By embracing the principles of resilience, consistency, and innovation, you can create a process that keeps your sales flowing and your business thriving for years to come. Like the ship that navigates through stormy seas and reaches its destination, your business can weather any challenge and continue moving forward toward its goals.

THE STORY OF MORNING BLISS

In the early days, Morning Bliss was nothing more than a small coffee shop, opened by a passionate couple, Jake and Lily. They had a dream: to create a space where people could escape the hustle of everyday life, sip on their favorite coffee, and feel as though they were part of something special. Jake and Lily poured all their time, energy, and savings into the business. They hand-picked the beans from local farmers, crafted a cozy environment, and ensured that every cup of coffee was made with love. But despite their passion and effort, the sales numbers didn't meet their expectations. They had opened their doors in a bustling city center, yet many potential customers walked by without a second glance.

They were facing real challenges. The competition was fierce. There were dozens of other coffee shops in the area, many of them offering similar products at competitive prices. And even though their coffee was of superior quality, they struggled to stand out. Customers would occasionally pop in, but no one stayed long enough to form a lasting connection. They were getting sales, but they weren't getting the loyalty they needed. Without customer loyalty, there was no guarantee of repeat sales, and without repeat sales, there would be no profit.

Jake spent many sleepless nights questioning whether they had made the right choice. He asked himself, "How do we make this work? How do we keep selling and make a profit, when everything feels like it's against us?"

That's when he realized the problem wasn't the product—it was the strategy. He needed to focus not just on selling a cup of coffee, but on building something bigger: a relationship with every customer that walked in the door.

STEP 1: UNDERSTAND THE LIFEBLOOD OF YOUR BUSINESS

In a crowded marketplace, it's not enough to simply have a great product. You need to have great relationships. Jake realized that the future of their business depended on building rapport with every person who walked through their door. The challenge was to turn these one-time visitors into repeat customers who would return, time and again, because of the connection they had formed with Morning Bliss.

It started with the simplest thing: remembering names. Jake began to make a habit of greeting every customer by name. It wasn't just a polite gesture—it was a deliberate attempt to create a personal bond. Every morning, he would stand behind the counter, look up from the register, and greet each customer with a warm, genuine smile. Sometimes, he'd remember small details from their last visit and ask about their day. He made sure that his interactions felt genuine and not transactional.

On a particularly busy morning, Jake noticed a regular customer, Sarah, coming in. She always ordered a cappuccino, but today, she seemed particularly tired, rubbing her eyes and yawning. Jake, sensing something was off, took a chance. He said, "Sarah, you look like you've had a long night. How about trying something stronger today—a double espresso with a bit of cinnamon to get you going?"

Sarah hesitated, but then smiled and said, "Sure, why not?" She tried it, and the next day, she returned to the shop with a big smile. "That espresso shot was exactly what I needed," she said. "I felt like a new person!"

Jake had made a connection with Sarah. He didn't just sell her a cup of coffee—he gave her an experience, something that helped her feel better in the moment. This was the foundation of the loyalty that would drivefuture sales.

STEP 2: CREATE REPEAT BUSINESS THROUGHCONSISTENCY

Jake and Lily understood that consistency was critical to keeping customers coming back. The coffee had to taste the same every time. The atmosphere had to remain cozy and welcoming. Customers needed to know that no matter when they walked in, they would get the same high-quality product and friendly service.

Lily took it upon herself to ensure that the customer experience was the same every time. She crafted a training manual for the baristas, setting the standard for how each coffee should be made, how each customer should be greeted, and how the store should feel. It became a mantra: Every cup, every time.

But even with this consistency, they knew they needed something more to ensure repeat business: a reason for customers to return regularly. That's when they implemented a loyalty program.

The program was simple: after buying ten cups of coffee, customers would receive a free one. But what Jake and Lily didn't realize at the time wasthat the program wasn't just about offering discounts—it was about reinforcing the relationship. It was a way to say, "We see you. We value you. And we want you to come back."

They introduced the loyalty cards with a bit of flair, handing them out with enthusiasm. Jake would personally explain the program to each customer, saying, "We're so happy you came by. Let's make sure you get rewarded for being such a great customer!"

A few months later, they saw a noticeable shift. The customers who had signed up for the loyalty program started returning more frequently. Their friends began visiting Morning Bliss too, and before long, the shop was buzzing with a constant stream of regulars.

STEP 3: INNOVATE AND ADAPT – ALWAYS STAYAHEAD OF THE CURVE

Consistency was key, but Jake and Lily knew they couldn't afford to be complacent. The coffee industry is dynamic—new trends emerge, customer preferences change, and competitors innovate. To keep their business growing, they had to adapt and innovate.

First, they introduced seasonal drinks. Pumpkin spice lattes in the fall, peppermint mochas during the holidays, and cold brews in the summer. These limited-time offerings not only kept the menu fresh, but they also created a sense of urgency—customers wanted to try these unique drinks before they disappeared.

They also introduced coffee tasting nights—an event where customers could come in, sample different beans, and learn more about the brewing process. These events were popular, attracting a new crowd who might not have visited otherwise. It wasn't just about coffee—it was about the experience.

Jake and Lily also realized that technology could play a huge role in their success. They created an online ordering system that allowed customers to place their orders ahead of time. This was especially helpful during the busy morning rush, and it helped the shop run more efficiently.

A social media strategy followed. They posted regular updates on Instagram and Facebook, showcasing new menu items, customer stories, and behind-the-scenes peeks into the shop. Every post was designed to remind their followers that they weren't just a coffee shop—they were a community.

The innovations didn't stop there. Jake and Lily continually sought feedback from their customers to stay ahead of the curve. They used surveys, talked to regulars, and watched industry trends to ensure they were always in the loop.

STEP 4: EMBRACE CUSTOMER FEEDBACK – THE KEY TO GROWTH

Jake and Lily knew that one of the best ways to improve was to listen. Feedback became their best friend. When customers voiced concerns—whether it was about a drink they didn't like or an experience they didn't enjoy—they took it seriously.

But they didn't just respond passively. Instead, they actively sought out feedback. They created a simple feedback form that was available in-store and online. They also asked customers directly, "What can we do better? How can we make your experience even more enjoyable?"

This feedback loop was invaluable. It allowed them to fix small issues before they became big problems and helped them refine their offerings. For instance, a few customers mentioned that they wished there were more vegan-friendly options on the menu. Jake and Lily took that to heart and introduced plant-based milk options, as well as a new line of vegan pastries. These changes not only met the needs of their existing customers, but they attracted a new customer base.

STEP 5: THE POWER OF MARKETING – PROMOTEAND SPREAD THE WORD

While customer loyalty and consistent service were vital, marketing was still essential to growing their reach. Jake and Lily understood that, to keepselling and increase profits, they needed to market Morning Bliss effectively. This didn't mean huge advertising budgets or flashy campaigns—it meant getting the word out in a strategic way.

They took advantage of local partnerships. They collaborated with nearby businesses, offering joint promotions and cross-promotion on social media. The more people they connected with, the more exposure they gained. They also implemented email marketing—sending out weekly newsletters that featured upcoming events, exclusive offers, and updates about their new menu items.

CONCLUSION

Today, Morning Bliss is not just a coffee shop—it's a beloved community hub. Jake and Lily's commitment to consistent service, personal connections, innovation, and active listening has allowed them to keep selling and increase their profits.

Through dedication, adaptability, and a constant drive to improve, they've created a brand that's both sustainable and profitable. And while the journey wasn't always easy, it has been a reminder that in business, perseverance and relationships are the key ingredients for success.

To keep selling and making a profit, you must be willing to put in the hard work, stay consistent, and adapt to ever-changing circumstances. The story of Morning Bliss teaches us that selling is more than a one-time transaction—it's about creating meaningful, lasting relationships that will keep your business thriving for years to come.

CHAPTER 15: LOYALTY PROGRAM

It's a quiet morning in the heart of a bustling city. A small, unassuming café sits nestled between towering buildings, a refuge for anyone in need of a moment of peace. The air is filled with the faint hum of the city outside, but inside, there's a comforting warmth that embraces every visitor. Soft jazz music plays in the background, and the rich, aromatic smell of freshly brewed coffee lingers in the air. It's a place that feels like home for many, a cozy corner where people come to escape the chaos of the world for just a few moments.

You've been coming to this café for months, maybe even longer. Each visit feels like a small ritual, a cherished part of your day. You've found your favorite seat by the window, where you can watch the world go by, sip on your cappuccino, and take a deep breath. The baristas know your name, your order, and sometimes even your mood. One morning, as you approach the counter, the barista looks up from behind the counter with a smile, her eyes twinkling with familiarity. "Cappuccino with extra foam?" she asks, before you can even speak. You smile back, surprised, but appreciative. She's right—it's exactly what you want today.

And then, she slides a small, elegant card across the counter to you. "This is our loyalty card," she says, with a hint of excitement in her voice. "After ten cups of coffee, you get one free."

At first, it seems like a simple gesture—a small token of

appreciation for your continued patronage. But as you walk back to your seat with the card in hand, you can't help but feel a little spark of something deeper. It's not just about the free coffee—it's about the feeling of being valued. You've been coming to this café for so long, and now, in a small way, they are acknowledging your loyalty. You're more than just a regular customer. You're part of something.

This small act, seemingly insignificant in the grand scheme of things, has just created a deeper connection between you and this café. And over time, as you visit more frequently, the loyalty card becomes a reminder of your relationship with the place. Every time you scan it, you feel a sense of accomplishment. Every sip of coffee seems sweeter because it's a tangible symbol of your ongoing connection to something that values you.

BUILDING TRUST AND RELATIONSHIPS

A loyalty program is far more than a transactional tool—it's a bridge that connects a business and its customers on a deeper level. When you offer a loyalty program, you are not simply giving out rewards or discounts. You are sending a powerful message: "We appreciate you, and we want to thank you for choosing us." That simple message can have an extraordinary impact on a customer's relationship with your brand.

Loyalty programs create a sense of belonging. They invite customers to become part of something bigger than just a business transaction. When done right, they transform a one-time purchase into a long-lasting relationship. A loyalty program is about more than keeping customers coming back—it's about creating an experience that makes them feel valued, respected, and appreciated. This chapter will explore how a well-designed loyalty program can turn your customers into passionate advocates for your brand.

WHY LOYALTY PROGRAMS MATTER

In a world where customer choices are endless, where every business isvying for attention, it's easy to feel like a small fish in a big pond. Whetheryou run a local café, a national retail chain, or an online marketplace, the competition is fierce. With the rise of e-commerce, online reviews, andendless options at customers' fingertips, businesses must find ways to stand out and foster relationships with their customers. This is where loyalty programs come in.

Loyalty programs are not just about giving discounts— they are about making customers feel valued. When customers feel valued, they are morelikely to return to your brand, purchase more often, and recommend youto others. Loyalty programs take your relationship with customers beyond the point of sale, encouraging them to engage with your brand on a deeper, more emotional level.

Research shows that loyal customers are more likely to make repeat purchases and spend more money over time. In fact, it's been found that loyal customers spend, on average, 67% more than new customers. Additionally, loyal customers are more likely to refer your business to friends and family, helping you build a community of brand advocates. This is the power of loyalty programs—they create an ecosystem where customers don't just buy from you; they champion your brand.

WHY WE STAY COMMITTED

To truly understand the power of loyalty programs, it's important to dive into the psychology behind them. What makes people want to return to a business time and time again? Why do customers go out of their way to be a part of a loyalty program? The answer lies in the deep-seated psychological principles that govern human behavior.

One of the most powerful motivators is the principle of reciprocity. This is the idea that when someone does something for us, we feel compelled to return the favor. In the case of loyalty programs, businesses give customers a reward or incentive for their loyalty—whether it's a free product, a discount, or an exclusive offer. This act of giving triggers the reciprocity principle, making customers feel as though they owe the business something in return. As a result, they are more likely to continue purchasing from the brand to "repay" that kindness.

Another psychological factor at play is the desire for progress. Loyalty programs often operate on a point system or a tiered structure, where customers earn points with each purchase that lead to a reward. This taps into the human need to make progress and achieve goals. Every time customers make a purchase and accumulate points, they feel a sense of accomplishment. They can see the fruits of their efforts and look forward to the reward that awaits them at the end.

Additionally, loyalty programs leverage social proof. When customers see others engaging with a brand's loyalty program, they are more likely to participate themselves. People tend to follow the actions of others, especially when they see those actions being rewarded. Social proof helps build trust and credibility, further encouraging customers to engage with the program.

Finally, loyalty programs create emotional connections. When a customer signs up for a program, they are not just looking for discounts—they are looking for a deeper connection with the brand. They want to feel special, recognized, and appreciated. When businesses provide personalized rewards or exclusive offers, they reinforce the idea that customers are unique and valued. This emotional connection is what turns a regular customer into a loyal advocate.

A STEP-BY-STEP GUIDE

Building a successful loyalty program requires more than just offering discounts. It's about designing a program that resonates with your customers and makes them feel like they are part of something special. Here's a step-by-step guide to creating a loyalty program that fosters long-term relationships and drives customer retention.

STEP 1: KNOW YOUR AUDIENCE

Before you design a loyalty program, it's essential to understand who your customers are, what they value, and what motivates them to engage with your brand. Are your customers motivated by discounts, exclusivity, or convenience? Do they appreciate personalized experiences, or are they more driven by the prospect of earning points? Understanding yourcustomer base is crucial for designing a program that speaks directly to their needs and desires.

You can gather insights into your customers by analyzing their purchasing behavior, conducting surveys, or simply observing patterns in their interactions with your business. The more you know about your audience, the better equipped you'll be to create a loyalty program that resonates with them.

STEP 2: DETERMINE YOUR REWARD STRUCTURE

The rewards you offer are the backbone of your loyalty program. But not all rewards are created equal. It's important to offer rewards that are both valuable to your customers and sustainable for your business. The goal is to create a reward system that encourages customers to return to your brand without undermining your bottom line.

Consider the types of rewards that would best resonate with your audience. Do they prefer discounts on future purchases, or would they appreciate free products or services? Some businesses offer tiered rewards, where customers can unlock bigger and better rewards as they make more purchases or engage with the brand. This encourages customers to keep coming back in order to reach the next level.

The rewards should be achievable, but not too easy. If the rewards are too easy to attain, customers may lose interest. On the other hand, if they are too difficult to reach, customers may feel discouraged and, subsequently, disengage. Striking the right balance is key.

STEP 3: MAKE IT EASY TO JOIN

A successful loyalty program should be easy to join and use. If the sign-up process is complicated or requires too much effort, customers may not bother. The more seamless and convenient you make the process, the more likely customers are to sign up and engage with the program.

Consider offering multiple ways for customers to join the program—whether through a website, mobile app, or in-store. Make sure the program is easy to track and redeem rewards, and ensure that the customer experience is smooth from start to finish.

STEP 4: PERSONALIZE THE EXPERIENCE

A great loyalty program isn't just about offering generic rewards—it's about making customers feel like they are receiving something special. Personalization is the key to creating an emotional connection with your customers. Use the data you have about your customers to tailor the rewards and experiences they receive. For example, if a customer frequently buys a certain product, offer them a discount on that item or provide exclusive access to related products.

Personalized offers make customers feel valued and appreciated, and they increase the likelihood that customers will engage with your program long-term.

STEP 5: COMMUNICATE REGULARLY

Once your loyalty program is up and running, it's important to keep your customers engaged. Regular communication helps remind them of the program and encourages them to continue participating. Send email updates about their points balance, exclusive offers, and new rewards. Use social media to promote the program and celebrate milestones. Regular touchpoints keep your brand top of mind and reinforce the emotional connection between you and your customers.

STEP 6: TRACK AND OPTIMIZE

Finally, it's important to track the success of your loyalty program and make adjustments as needed. Analyze customer participation rates, redemption rates, and overall sales to determine how effective the program is. Solicit feedback from customers to identify areas for improvement. By continuously optimizing your loyalty program, you can ensure that it remains relevant and valuable to your customers.

CASE STUDY: STARBUCKS REWARDS

One of the most successful loyalty programs in recent history is the Starbucks Rewards program. With over 24 million members, Starbucks has created a loyalty program that goes beyond simply offering discounts. The program offers customers the ability to earn stars with each purchase, which can be redeemed for free drinks, food, and exclusive offers.

But what makes Starbucks Rewards truly successful is its seamless integration with the company's mobile app. Customers can order ahead, pay via the app, and track their rewards in real-time. The program also offers personalized rewards based on customers' purchasing habits, making them feel like the company truly understands their preferences.

Starbucks has also used its loyalty program to build a community. The program encourages customers to engage with the brand beyond just making purchases. By offering rewards for social media interactions, such as sharing posts or writing reviews, Starbucks has created a sense of belonging among its members. The loyalty program is more than just a transactional tool—it's a way for customers to feel like they are part of a larger community.

CONCLUSION

In the end, a loyalty program is about more than just keeping customers coming back—it's about creating lasting relationships. It's about making customers feel valued, appreciated, and part of something meaningful. When customers feel like they are a part of your brand, they are more likely to stay loyal, refer others, and spend more money over time. By designing a loyalty program that is personalized, easy to use, and emotionally engaging, you can foster deeper connections with your customers and build a brand that they are proud to support.

Loyalty programs are not just about rewards—they are about building trust, creating an emotional connection, and turning customers into passionate advocates for your brand. When done right, they can transform a one-time transaction into a lifelong relationship.

CHAPTER 16: MEMBERSHIP PROGRAM

In today's rapidly evolving business landscape, companies are increasingly recognizing the monumental shift from simple transactional exchanges to the development of long-term, value-driven partnerships with their customers. While traditional business models have primarily focused on the act of selling a product or service—an interaction that, though important, is often short-lived and one-dimensional—the more progressive and enduring approach is one that seeks to build lasting relationships. This is where a truly transformative shift occurs: the move from merely providing a product to fostering an ongoing, mutually beneficial connection with customers. Rather than just focusing on a singlepurchase or service rendered, businesses are moving toward creating deep, meaningful bonds that extend well beyond the transaction.

The difference between a transactional relationship and a relational one cannot be overstated. A transactional interaction might be characterized by a single sale, a quick exchange of goods or services for money, and little emotional or personal connection. These relationships, while essential for generating revenue in the short term, rarely inspire loyalty or customer retention. On the other hand, a relationship-driven approach is all about developing an emotional investment and creating a sense of belonging for the customer. This strategy focuses on building long-term connections, fostering trust, and offering exclusive value that transcends mere monetary exchanges. In this chapter, we are going to delve deeply into one of the most powerful tools available to businesses aiming to nurture such valuable relationships with their customers: the membership program.

At its core, a membership program is far more than a straightforward offering of discounts, loyalty points, or rewards—though these can certainly be components of an effective program. The essence of a successful membership program lies in its ability to create a sense of community and exclusivity, where customers feel not just like buyers, but like integral members of something bigger. This shift is monumental. Instead of merely being recipients of a transaction, customers are invited into an exclusive world—one where they are valued, recognized, and made to feel like part of a dynamic, thriving community.

But why is this so important? Why should businesses care about turning a simple customer transaction into a deep, value-driven membership experience? The answer lies in the psychology of human connection. People, at their core, crave relationships. We are wired to seek belonging and community, and this desire doesn't stop when we make a purchase. In fact, the opposite is true. Once we've bought a product or service from a company, we want to feel like our decision was validated, that we are not just another sale, but a valued part of something larger. A well-structured membership program taps directly into this need for community and connection, and in doing so, it transforms customers from passive participants to active brand advocates.

When executed properly, a membership program does more than offer customers financial incentives or rewards; it enriches their lives by offering them valuable experiences and emotional rewards that go far beyond what a simple transaction could provide. Imagine, for a moment, a customer who isn't just receiving a discount on their next purchase, but is being invited to exclusive events, gaining early access to new products or services, and receiving personalized content or experiences that speak directly to their needs and desires. This type of engagement creates a bond—a sense of emotional investment—that turns a one-time buyer into a loyal member of your brand's inner circle. It's this feeling of belonging, of being recognized and valued, that transforms a customer from a mere consumer into a true brand advocate.

The journey of building such a program is an art form in itself, one that requires a deep understanding of both the emotional and practical aspects of customer relationships. It's about carefully curating experiences, rewards, and interactions that make customers feel genuinely valued, heard, and appreciated. But there's more to it than just offering perks. A truly successful membership program involves a deeper level of engagement—one that speaks to the heart of human motivation and creates a dynamic, evolving relationship between brand and customer.

In the following pages, we will explore the various facets of creating a powerful membership program, examining everything from its psychological underpinnings to the logistical steps involved in its design and execution. We'll discuss the art of curating experiences that go beyond simple rewards, and the importance of personalization in making each customer feel like a unique and valued part of your community. We will also look at the long-term benefits that come from developing a membership program that not only keeps customers engaged, but transforms them into passionate advocates who will go on to help drive your brand's success.

Understanding the psychology behind customer loyalty is a

critical part of this discussion. By diving into the underlying motivations that drive customer behavior, we can better understand how to craft a program that truly resonates with individuals on an emotional level. We'll also address the importance of exclusivity—why being part of an "inner circle" can make customers feel both special and deeply connected to the brand. This sense of exclusivity is not just about offering a select group of people special privileges, but about creating a space where members feel recognized and valued for their participation in the brand's ecosystem.

Furthermore, we will examine how a well-crafted membership program can benefit not only your customers but also your business. When executed thoughtfully, a membership program becomes a powerful tool for customer retention, brand advocacy, and long-term revenue growth. It's an investment in building a community of loyal customers who are not just interested in the products you sell, but in the experiences you offerand the values you represent.

THE BIRTH OF MEMBERSHIP PROGRAMS

Before we dive into the mechanics of a membership program, let's explore the rich history of one of the most successful membership-driven brandsin the world—Starbucks. It's not just a coffee shop; it's a global brand thathas turned the simple act of buying a cup of coffee into an experience, a lifestyle, and a sense of community.

Starbucks started as a small coffee roaster in Seattle, catering to a nichemarket of coffee connoisseurs who appreciated high-quality beans. But it wasn't until the company realized that it wasn't just coffee that people were after; it was the experience. It was the third place—somewhere between home and work—where people could relax, connect, and enjoy a ritual. But how could Starbucks foster that sense of community in a world where people were becoming increasingly busy and isolated? The answer was simple, yet revolutionary: the membership program.

They started offering a loyalty card. At first, it was a modest attempt to get people to come back more often, but it evolved into a full-blown membership program, where customers could earn rewards and enjoy exclusive perks. More than just a card with points, Starbucks turned the program into a platform for customers to feel like they were part of something larger—a community of like-minded coffee lovers. Members could earn free drinks, get early access to new products, and participate in members-only events. They were no longer customers; they were members of the Starbucks family.

As this program grew, so did the bond between the brand and its customers. What started as a simple transactional reward, became a deeper and a more emotional connection. Members weren't just buying coffee; they were becoming part of a culture, a movement. And this transformation is what any business can replicate if it understands the true potential of a membership program.

WHY MEMBERSHIP PROGRAMS WORK

At its core, the success of a membership program isn't just about the rewards or the special deals. It's about belonging. Humans are social creatures, and we have an innate desire to be part of something bigger than ourselves. We crave connection, recognition, and a sense of identity. A membership program taps into these deep-seated needs by offering a sense of exclusivity and community.

Imagine this: You're a regular customer at your favorite boutique. You love the products, you enjoy the customer service, and you've been coming back time and time again. One day, the store owner offers you amembership card. The card isn't just a discount card; it's an invitation into an exclusive group. Members get first access to sales, personalized recommendations, and invitations to VIP events. It's not just about the perks—it's about the fact that you've been chosen to be a part of something special. That feeling of being singled out, of being a "member" of an elite community, is priceless.

For businesses, this sense of belonging creates a bond that transcends amere transactional relationship. Customers don't just come for the product or service; they come for the experience of being part of something exclusive. This deeper connection makes them more likely to return, more likely to recommend the business to others, and more likely to remain loyal—even when competitors offer similar products or services.

CREATING EXCLUSIVITY

Humans are wired to seek out what is rare or exclusive. This is why luxurybrands, for example, don't just sell products—they sell exclusivity. Think of high-end fashion labels or expensive jewelry brands. It's not just about the quality of the product; it's about the status and identity that comes withowning something that's rare. The same principle applies to membership programs. When you create a sense of exclusivity around your business, your customers will feel like they are part of something special.

Take Costco, for example. The warehouse club has turned

the idea of exclusivity into a business model. In order to shop at Costco, you have to become a member—paying an annual fee for the privilege of shopping there. And while the savings and deals are a big draw, the real value comes from the exclusivity of the experience. You feel like you are part of an elite group of savvy shoppers who know the secret to getting high-quality products at a fraction of the cost. You aren't just buying in bulk; you're buying into a way of life, a club that's reserved for those who know how to get the best deals.

Creating this sense of exclusivity doesn't always require charging a membership fee, though. It could be as simple as offering early access to sales, limited-edition products, or members-only events. The key is to make your members feel that they have access to something others don't. That exclusivity taps into the desire to be part of a select group, and when done right, it transforms your membership program from a transactional tool into an emotional experience.

PROVIDING REAL, TANGIBLE VALUE

While exclusivity and belonging are important, the success of any membership program hinges on the value it provides. You can create all the exclusivity and emotional connection in the world, but if your membership program doesn't provide real, tangible benefits, it will fall flat. Customers will quickly realize that the perks aren't worth the investment, and your program will lose steam.

So what makes a membership program valuable? First and foremost, it's about offering personalization. The more personalized the experience, the more valuable it feels. Think about Amazon Prime. Yes, it offers free shipping, but it also provides members with exclusive access to Prime Video, Prime Music, and other perks. The real value is in the convenience and personalization that comes with the membership. Amazon knows what you like and what you buy. That's why they tailor their offers to you. This is what makes the program invaluable—it is designed specifically for you.

Personalization doesn't have to be complex. It could be as simple as a birthday gift for members, a customized shopping experience, or a recommendation engine based on past purchases. By providing value that speaks directly to the needs and desires of your customers, you create a program that's not just beneficial—it's indispensable.

CONSISTENCY AND TRUST

The beauty of a membership program is that it's not just a short-term reward system; it's a long-term investment in building customer loyalty. But for that loyalty to stick, you need to offer consistency. Customers need to know that the value they signed up for will remain steady over time. Whether it's access to exclusive events, discounts, or products, members need to feel that the benefits of their membership are reliable and consistent.

Think about the way Apple handles its membership programs, especially in relation to Apple Music or iCloud. Customers aren't just subscribing for one month—they're committing to an ongoing service. Apple ensures that the experience remains seamless, that the content remains relevant, and that the value is consistently high. They build trust with their members by offering top-quality experiences every single time.

Consistency also applies to how businesses handle customer service. If a member has a question or concern, how quickly and effectively do you respond? Are you there for them when they need help, or are they left feeling like just another number in a queue? Building trust means showing up time and time again, being there for your customers when it counts.

TURNING MEMBERS INTO ADVOCATES

Once you've established a solid membership program that offers exclusivity, value, and consistency, the next step is to turn your members into advocates. One of the most powerful tools in any business's arsenal is word-of-mouth marketing. When your members love what you do, they'll naturally want to tell others about it. But how do you encourage them to spread the word?

This is where referral bonuses or advocate programs come into play. When a member refers a friend or family member to your membership program, reward them with additional perks. It could be extra points, exclusive access to products, or even a free month of service. Not only does this incentivize your members to spread the word, but it also deepens their connection to your brand.

Think about how Dropbox grew its user base. The company initially offered free space to existing users for every new user they referred. This small, but powerful, incentive led to exponential growth. Suddenly, users weren't just customers—they were active participants in the company's success. They had a personal stake in spreading the word, and in return, they were rewarded with benefits that mattered to them.

THE FUTURE OF MEMBERSHIP PROGRAMS

As technology continues to evolve, so too will membership programs. Today, businesses have access to vast amounts of data and the ability to create highly personalized and dynamic experiences for their members. AI and machine learning will continue to play a role in this evolution, allowing businesses to anticipate customer needs and deliver even more tailored experiences.

Additionally, as more businesses move online, membership programs will evolve to include virtual communities and digital experiences that make members feel connected no matter where they are. The ability to create virtual events, live streams, and online-exclusive offers will continue to redefine what it means to be a member of a brand.

CONCLUSION

The true magic of a membership program lies in its ability to foster long-term relationships. It's more than just a way to reward loyal customers; it's a way to make your customers feel valued, heard, and connected to something greater than themselves. When done right, a membership program can turn ordinary transactions into extraordinary experiences, creating a community that is passionate, engaged, and loyal.

Like the greatest brands in the world, your business has the potential to turn customers into lifelong members—people who don't just buy your products, but who identify with your brand and champion it to others. The membership program is a powerful tool, but it's the connections you build with your members that will turn them into advocates, fans, and loyal customers for life.

And that's the real power of membership. It's not just about the rewards—it's about creating a relationship that lasts, that transcends the transaction, and that turns a simple customer into a lifelong champion of your brand.

CHAPTER 17: HOW TO ACQUIRE MONTHLY SUBSCRIPTIONS FROM CUSTOMERS

It was a crisp autumn morning when Caroline, the owner of a small but rapidly growing boutique fitness studio, sat at her desk, staring at her computer screen. Her mind raced with a mixture of excitement and frustration. She had spent years building her business, pouring her heart and soul into every class, every client, and every interaction. She had created a studio that her customers loved—an environment where they felt empowered, supported, and challenged. But despite all her hard work, there was something that still kept her awake at night: the unpredictability of her revenue.

Caroline had grown her customer base by offering high-quality, personalized workout experiences. Her clients loved her; they raved about the classes, the energy, and the sense of community. But there was one issue: her income wasn't as stable as it could be. Some customers came religiously, attending multiple classes per week. Others came once in a while, buying bulk packs of classes but rarely using them. The lack of consistency in attendance meant that she couldn't predict how much money would flow into the business each month. Some months, she had too many clients, and others, the classes barely met the minimum requirements to cover the operating expenses.

It was during one of these restless nights that Caroline stumbled upon an article that would change her business forever.

As she scrolled through hersocial media feed, she noticed a post about the growing trend of subscription-based businesses. It struck her immediately: why wasn't she offering her clients a monthly subscription? After all, people subscribed to everything these days—magazines, meal kits, streaming services, even personal grooming services. Why not fitness?

But the more she thought about it, the more she realized that acquiring monthly subscriptions from customers would require more than just offering a simple membership. It wasn't just about securing consistent revenue—it was about creating something that resonated with her customers on a deeper level. How could she design a subscription model that would add real value, enhance her clients' experience, and ensure that the business could grow in a sustainable way? She had to think strategically and carefully, and this is where the real journey began.

THE PROBLEM OF UNPREDICTABILITY

In the early days of her studio, Caroline's business model was simple. She offered a pay-per-class structure or a discounted bulk class package. Onthe surface, it made sense. Her customers paid for classes whenever they attended, and those who bought bulk packs saved money in the long run. It worked fine for a while. The regulars attended their classes, the occasional visitors came when they could, and the revenue was relatively steady.

But the cracks began to show. Caroline had a group of loyal clients who came multiple times a week, but there was also a significant number ofpeople who would buy class packs and use only a fraction of the sessions. This created revenue fluctuations that left Caroline constantly wondering how much she could depend on from month to month. Some months, she had a solid income; others, it was far from guaranteed. She couldn't accurately predict what would happen next month or next week, and that lack of certainty made it impossible for her to plan.

Caroline knew that if she wanted to scale the business, she needed a more reliable income stream. Her dream wasn't just to survive; it was to thrive. She wanted to grow her business, hire more staff, expand her offerings, and create a lasting impact on her clients' lives. But to do that, she needed predictable cash flow—something she could count on month after month.

That was the point when Caroline started thinking seriously about monthly subscriptions. If she could offer a plan that allowed her clients to commit to her studio on a monthly basis, it would give her the financial stability she needed to expand her business. But how would she make this appealing to her clients? After all, people didn't always like being locked into contracts, and they certainly didn't want to pay for something they weren't going to use. This was the real challenge.

CREATING A MEMBERSHIP MODEL

As Caroline researched subscription models, she realized that the concept wasn't new. Across various industries, businesses were shifting toward subscription-based offerings, from gyms to meal kits to even online content platforms like Netflix. This new model was not just about offering a product or service—it was about creating an ongoing relationship with the customer, one built on trust, value, and commitment.

However, Caroline's mind wasn't just focused on revenue generation. She was thinking about her customers. She didn't want her clients to feel like they were simply signing up for another recurring payment. She wanted them to feel that the monthly subscription was something worth their time, energy, and, yes, money. It had to be more than just a payment plan—it had to be an investment in their health, well-being, and personal growth.

She began to ask herself important questions: What did her customers want? Why did they keep coming back to her studio? What could she offer that would make them excited about a monthly commitment?

Caroline's first step was to divide her customer base into two distinct groups: the loyal, frequent visitors, and the more occasional clients. These two groups had different needs, and she realized that her subscription offering should cater to both.

- **The Regulars:** These were the clients who attended her classes ona near-daily basis. They were deeply committed to their fitness journeys and made working out a priority. For them, Caroline created an "Unlimited Access" plan, which allowed them to attend any class, at any time, without having to pay for each session individually. These regulars were willing to invest in their fitness, and they wanted the flexibility to attend as often as they wished. The "Unlimited Access" plan felt like an obvious fit for them.

- **The Occasional Clients:** Then there were the clients who didn't come as frequently. They weren't ready to commit to a full membership, but they still wanted to take part in classes without feeling restricted. For these individuals, Caroline introduced a "10- Class Per Month" subscription. This plan allowed them to take up to ten classes per month, which was perfect for those who didn't have time to attend multiple times a week. It gave them flexibility without the pressure of paying for unused classes, and it offered a more budget-friendly option for people with busy schedules.

- After finalizing the two membership tiers, Caroline spent time refining the pricing to ensure it was competitive yet sustainable. She also added a few enticing perks to each subscription level: priority booking for popular classes, access to exclusive members-only events, and discounts on merchandise or workshops. These extra benefits made the subscription feel like a true value proposition for her clients.

MARKETING THE SUBSCRIPTION MODEL

Once the membership model was designed, Caroline's next hurdle was to market it. She knew her current customers were loyal, but how could she convince them to take the leap and sign up for a subscription? She had to think beyond traditional marketing tactics and create a narrative that wouldresonate deeply with her clients.

- **Email Campaigns:** Caroline began by sending out a series of emails to her existing clients. She framed the subscription model

not just as a way to pay less, but as an opportunity to make fitnessa consistent part of their lives. The messaging was personalized, highlighting how regular workouts could improve their physical and mental health. She also emphasized the exclusivity of the new subscription model—this wasn't just another generic offering; it was a carefully crafted plan designed to meet their needs. She used testimonials from her most loyal clients to create social proof and show potential subscribers how valuable the new model could be.

- **Social Media Campaigns:** Caroline took to her Instagram, which already had a growing following. She created a series of posts and stories to build anticipation for the subscription launch. She used countdowns, sneak peeks, and behind-the-scenes looks at the new perks and benefits that came with the subscription model. She also created videos showing happy clients using their new membership cards and enjoying their benefits. These posts were interactive, asking followers to comment on how much they would love an unlimited fitness plan. She included special offers for the first 50 people who signed up, creating a sense of urgency.

- **Referral Program:** To further incentivize her loyal clients, Caroline introduced a referral program. For every new member who signed up through a current client's referral, the referring client would receive a free month of classes or other perks. This was a powerful way to generate organic growth, as clients who were already happy with her services would bring in friends and family who might not have otherwise considered the subscription.

- **In-Studio Sign-Ups:** Finally, Caroline set up a dedicated membership desk inside the studio where clients could sign up on the spot. This made the process feel seamless and allowed Caroline to personally explain the benefits of the new model to anyone who had questions. This personalized touch also ensured that potential subscribers felt heard and valued.

THE POWER OF EXCLUSIVITY AND COMMUNITY

One of the most unexpected outcomes of introducing a subscription model was how much it enhanced the sense of community at her studio. As Caroline's subscription numbers grew, she began to notice a stronger bond between her clients. It wasn't just about the fitness classes anymore; it was about belonging to something special.

Caroline decided to leverage this sense of community by hosting exclusive, members-only events. These events ranged from fitness challenges to wellness workshops to social gatherings outside of the gym. These events gave clients an opportunity to connect with each other, network, and share their fitness journeys. The goal wasn't just to work out together; it was to build a supportive, encouraging environment where members could feel a deep connection to one another.

As the months went on, Caroline's clients didn't just feel like they were paying for access to classes; they felt like they were part of an exclusive family. They had invested in the studio's vision, and in return, they were receiving not just fitness classes, but a holistic experience.

A SUSTAINABLE BUSINESS MODEL

By the end of her first quarter with the subscription model in place, Caroline saw impressive results. Her revenue had increased by 40%, and her client retention rate had skyrocketed. The predictability of her monthly income allowed her to plan for the future with confidence. She was able to hire more trainers, offer additional services like private coaching, and even expand her studio to accommodate the growing demand.

Most importantly, her clients were happier. The flexibility of the subscription model made them feel more in control of their fitness journey, while the sense of community and exclusivity created a stronger emotionalconnection to the studio.

CREATING A VALUE-DRIVEN SUBSCRIPTION

Caroline's journey serves as a powerful and inspiring example of how, when implemented thoughtfully and strategically, monthly subscription models can revolutionize a business. It's easy to view subscriptions as merely a transactional relationship—a recurring payment every month fora product or service—but Caroline's story goes far beyond that narrow understanding. Her success didn't come from simply locking customers into automatic billing cycles; it came from focusing on creating authentic, lasting value that met the needs of her customers in meaningful ways. In the process, she transformed her business from one-time transactions into a sustainable, growth-focused enterprise powered by loyal, long-term subscribers.

The first key to Caroline's success was her ability to listen attentively to her customers. In an era where personalization and understanding are critical, Caroline made it a priority to actively engage with her audience, learning not just about their immediate needs but also their long-term goals, preferences, and desires. This wasn't about offering a generic product or service that could be sold to anyone. Instead, she took the time to understand her customers deeply, tailoring her offerings to align with their specific lifestyles, challenges, and aspirations.

In addition to personalized service, Caroline recognized that flexibility was paramount. People's lives, habits, and preferences are always evolving, and a subscription model that doesn't adapt to these shifts is destined to fail. By offering options that allowed customers to modify their subscription plans, pause their services when needed, or switch between different offerings, Caroline built a level of trust and goodwill that encouraged people to stick with her business for the long haul. Flexibility wasn't just a nice perk; it became a cornerstone of her customer experience, fostering a sense of ease and confidence that kept people coming back month after month.

But perhaps the most significant aspect of Caroline's approach was her commitment to building a genuine community. She didn't view her customers as faceless individuals who were simply paying for her product or service. Instead, she saw them as integral members of a thriving ecosystem—people whose input, feedback, and engagement could help shape the future of her business. She created platforms for open dialogue, hosted events where subscribers could interact with each other, and provided exclusive content and experiences that made her customers feel like they were part of something bigger than just a transaction. This sense of belonging, of being valued as more than just a revenue stream, was something that drove deeper emotional connections and a higher level of engagement with her business.

The beauty of a subscription model, whether you're running a fitness studio, a digital service, a coffee shop, or any other type of business, lies in its ability to offer clients something far more meaningful than just a product or service. It's not about a one-time sale; it's about providing consistent, ongoing value that reinforces a deeper relationship with your customers. People crave consistency, especially in today's fast-paced world. Subscriptions give them a reliable source of value—whether that'sa workout routine that helps them stay fit, a monthly delivery of their favorite products, or a service that makes their lives easier. With regular and predictable engagement, customers are less likely to drift away or be tempted by competitors because they've built a bond with your brand, grounded in trust and ongoing value.

On the business side, a well-executed subscription model doesn't just benefit your customers; it provides crucial advantages to you as a business owner. The most obvious of these is financial stability. Monthly subscriptions create a predictable revenue stream that makes it easier to manage cash flow and plan for the future. This stability also allows you to focus on long-term growth rather than being caught in the endless cycle of chasing one-time sales. You can reinvest in your business, expand your offerings, and continually improve your products or services because you have the certainty of recurring income.

Moreover, the growth potential of a subscription-based model is vast.

Once you've cultivated a loyal base of subscribers, it becomes easier to scale your business. Each new subscriber adds to your existing community, creating a snowball effect that enhances your brand's reach and influence. The more value you provide, the more likely your customers are to recommend your services to others, which can fuel organic growth and expand your market reach without the need for massive marketing budgets.

Caroline's story also demonstrates the power of retention.

In many industries, customer acquisition can be an expensive and time-consuming process. But with a subscription model, the emphasis shifts from constantly finding new customers to nurturing the ones you already have. Retaining customers not only saves money but also builds a stable, repeatable revenue stream that can weather economic fluctuations. The longer customers stay, the more valuable they become, and in Caroline's case, this retention created a powerful feedback loop of growth and success.

But perhaps most importantly, Caroline's success shows that when you create a business model that is built on customer trust, value, and community, you aren't just building a business—you're building a loyal following that is genuinely invested in your success. This kind of support extends far beyond the transactional nature of a sale. It turns customers into advocates, into ambassadors for your brand, and into people who are excited to see your business thrive because they feel connected to its mission and purpose.

CHAPTER 18: HOW DO YOU THINK CUSTOMERS WILL STAY WITH YOU FOREVER?

The world of business is full of stories—some of triumph, others of struggle—but few stories carry as much weight as the ones where small businesses defy the odds and establish enduring, loyal customer bases. One of the most compelling stories I know is that of Clara, the owner of a small, local bookstore that survived—and even thrived—during an era when many other brick-and-mortar stores were closing down. Her success didn't lie in extravagant marketing campaigns or deep-pocketed investments. Instead, it came down to one simple truth: she understood the power of relationships, the value of creating meaningful experiences, and the importance of making customers feel like they were part of something larger than a mere transaction.

Let me take you into the world of Clara's bookstore, because it holds the keys to understanding why some businesses seem to have customers who stay forever, while others struggle to keep anyone coming back.

THE BEGINNINGS OF CLARA'S BOOKSTORE

Clara's bookstore wasn't always a beacon of success. In fact, when she opened it, the odds were stacked against her. We're talking about a small, independent bookstore, nestled between two chain stores, and at a time when online shopping was beginning to take over. In the early years, she had trouble competing with Amazon's vast inventory and the allure of one-click shopping. She knew that her business was fighting an uphill battle, and it was only a matter of time before she might have to close her doors.

But Clara was determined. She had a passion for books, and she believed in the power of the written word to bring people together, to make them think, feel, and understand the world in ways that digital screens could not. However, Clara's love for literature was not enough. She needed something more. She needed a vision—a way to offer people something they couldn't get from an online retailer or a chain store. She realized that in order to stand out, she had to give people an experience. An experience that was more than just browsing books.

At the heart of her business strategy was the realization that customers weren't just buying books—they were buying a connection. They were buying into a world that felt personal, warm, and inviting. Clara wasn't just selling stories; she was selling an emotional experience, a sense of belonging that no other store could replicate. Slowly, she started to turn her bookstore into more than just a place to shop. She made it a place where people could gather, converse, and connect. She knew that for her to survive, her customers had to become more than just patrons. They had to become part of a larger narrative—one that made them want to come back, not just for the books, but for the entire experience she provided.

THE HEART OF CUSTOMER LOYALTY

It didn't take long for Clara to understand that the key to her bookstore's success was relationships. Real, meaningful relationships that went beyond the transaction. She didn't see her customers as people coming in to buy a book and leave. She saw them as individuals with their own lives, their own stories, and their own needs. And every time someone walked through her door, Clara knew that she had an opportunity to make them feel valued.

One such customer was Sarah, a young woman who came into the store one Friday afternoon in search of a birthday gift for her mother. Sarah was a busy professional, and like many people, she didn't have much time to shop. She wasn't sure exactly what she was looking for, but she knew that her mother loved reading historical fiction, particularly novels set in the early 1900s. Clara took note of Sarah's stress and confusion and decided to do more than just offer a book. She wanted to offer a solution, a gift that would truly connect with Sarah's mother.

Instead of leading Sarah to the bestsellers, Clara took her down a quiet aisle of vintage books, books that were not only rare but also meaningful. There, nestled between the dusty shelves, was a collection of historical fiction novels from the early 1900s that perfectly matched Sarah's mother's taste. Sarah's eyes widened with delight as Clara handed her a novel, explaining the significance of the story and how it connected with the period Sarah's mother loved so much.

Sarah bought the book and left the store feeling both relieved and grateful. She didn't just buy a book; she bought a piece of her mother's past, a connection that went far deeper than just pages and ink. But the story didn't end there. A few weeks later, Sarah returned to Clara's bookstore, not because she needed to buy something, but because she wanted to talk. And then, a month later, she brought her mother in. The two of them became regulars, not just as customers but as members of a growing community that Clara was cultivating.

This is where the magic happens: when a business owner takes the time to understand their customers' needs on a deeper level and connects with them in a way that goes beyond a simple transaction. Clara didn't just sell Sarah a book. She made her feel understood. And that understanding is what turned Sarah into a loyal customer.

KNOWING YOUR CUSTOMERS

The key to creating lasting relationships with your customers is personalization. When you make the effort to truly understand your customers—when you get to know them on a deeper level—you open the door to something powerful: loyalty. Personalization doesn't just mean addressing customers by name; it means recognizing their preferences, anticipating their needs, and offering them something that speaks directly to them.

Clara wasn't content to just serve the same customers over and over. She wanted to understand them. Over time, she learned that certain customers preferred specific genres of books, others liked to be invited to special events, and some came in just for the camaraderie of the bookstore atmosphere. Clara knew when to offer a suggestion, when to give space, and when to initiate a conversation. She made her customers feel seen and heard in a way that other stores simply couldn't.

This level of personalization is what sets businesses apart. It's easy for a large chain store or an online retailer to become a faceless entity. But a small business owner like Clara can offer something special: they can make their customers feel like they're part of something unique. When you take the time to connect with people on a personal level, you're not just selling a product—you're building a relationship.

GOING BEYOND THE PRODUCT

The next lesson Clara learned was that businesses don't just survive on products—they survive on experiences. What's the difference between a customer who buys something and a customer who keeps coming back? The experience. Think about your own life. How many times have you walked into a store, purchased an item, and left, never to return? Now, think about the businesses that you return to time and time again. It's not because of the product alone. It's because of the experience they provide—the ambiance, the customer service, and the feeling that you get when you engage with them.

For Clara, creating memorable experiences meant offering more than just books. It meant hosting book clubs, offering author readings, and creating an inviting atmosphere where people could relax and talk about the books they loved. She started to host themed events like "Vintage Book Evenings" or "Historical Fiction Nights," where customers could come, share their favorite books, and discuss their thoughts with fellow readers. It became less about the books themselves and more about the sense of belonging that these events fostered.

When customers walk into a business, they want more than just a product—they want an experience. And that experience should make them feel something. Whether it's the warmth of the store, the quality of the service, or the sense of community, an unforgettable experience keeps people coming back. In Clara's case, it was the way her bookstore made people feel—like they belonged to something special.

STAYING RELEVANT TO YOUR CUSTOMERS

The world changes, and so do your customers. If you want them to stay with you forever, you have to evolve with them. Clara's bookstore didn't remain static. She continually assessed the needs and wants of her customers and adjusted accordingly. When she noticed a growing interest in local authors, she created a section dedicated to showcasing their work. When her customers started asking for more diverse genres, she expanded her offerings. She paid attention to the subtle shifts in her customers' preferences and responded in a way that kept them engaged and excitedabout coming back.

Adapting isn't just about keeping up with trends; it's about responding to the ever-changing landscape of customer desires. If Clara had remained stuck in her original model, only offering the same selection of books year after year, she would have lost customers to newer, more innovative businesses. But because she was always adapting—because she was always thinking about how to make her bookstore better, more interesting, and more aligned with her customers' needs—she was able to maintainher relevance in a rapidly changing world.

A SIMPLE, YET POWERFUL TOOL

The final piece of the puzzle that Clara understood was appreciation. People want to feel valued. It's a simple concept, yet it's often overlooked. Clara made a point of showing her customers that she appreciated their support. She did this in many ways—by remembering their names, by asking about their families, by offering them exclusive deals or early access to events. But the most powerful way Clara showed appreciation was through her actions.

She didn't just take her customers' money and run. She took the time to thank them, to make them feel special, and to go the extra mile. This wasn't just about customer service; it was about creating a culture of gratitude. Clara's customers knew that their loyalty mattered, and as a result, they were more than happy to return the favor.

Appreciation is one of the most powerful tools you have to keep customers coming back. A simple "thank you" can go a long way. But it's more than just words—it's about showing your customers that they are valued and that their loyalty means something.

THE LEGACY OF CUSTOMER LOYALTY

Clara's bookstore wasn't just another shop tucked away in a quiet corner of town—it was a sanctuary, a haven in the midst of a world rapidly changing under the weight of online shopping and the dominance of corporate retail giants. In a time when convenience and low prices often overshadowed the value of human connection, Clara's bookstore flourished in ways that many thought impossible. It wasn't the bestseller list or the deeply discounted prices that set her apart. It was something far more profound: Clara understood the timeless and transformative power of relationships.

Her business didn't just exist to sell books. It existed to foster connections, to nurture a sense of belonging, and to create an environment where customers felt like they were more than just faceless transactions. People didn't just walk into Clara's store to purchase a novel or pick up the latest bestseller; they came for something far more intangible, something they couldn't find in the cold, impersonal world of online shopping or chain stores. They came for a sense of community, for a place where they could feel valued, understood, and appreciated. It was the human touch—the personal relationships—that made Clara's bookstore a place of significance.

What Clara did differently was simple yet profound: she created an experience that went beyond the mere exchange of goods for money. She built an atmosphere where people were not just seen as customers, but as individuals with unique stories, passions, and needs. Her customers weren't just buying books— they were investing in a connection, a bond that transcended the material transaction. In a world increasingly dominated by algorithms and automated systems, Clara's customers felt that they mattered. They were heard. They were understood. And most importantly, they were valued.

In Clara's world, each interaction was an opportunity to deepen the relationship. She took the time to learn her customers' names, their preferences, and their interests. She didn't just recommend books based on bestsellers or trends; she recommended books that resonated with her customers' personal journeys, books that spoke to their souls. The conversations that took place within the walls of her bookstore weren't transactional—they were meaningful exchanges between two people who truly cared about one another. Clara was more than just a bookstore owner; she was a trusted friend, a confidant, and a guide. Her customers knew that when they walked through her doors, they weren't just entering a store—they were entering a space where they could be themselves, free from judgment and pressure.

This is the secret to building a business that endures. It's not about competing with prices or keeping up with the latest trends. It's about creating an experience that makes your customers feel truly seen, heard, and appreciated. It's about forming relationships that extend far beyond the exchange of money. It's about evolving alongside your customers, understanding their changing needs and desires, and showing them, time and again, that they matter—not just as customers, but as human beings.

The key is in making your customers feel like they are a part of somethingbigger, something lasting, something that matters. When you invest in relationships, you build a foundation of trust that can weather any storm. Your customers become more than just patrons—they become your advocates, your supporters, and your friends. They'll return, time and again, because they know that in your business, they are valued for who they are, not just what they can buy.

When you focus on building relationships, the rewards are far greater than mere customer loyalty. You create a legacy of trust and connection thattranscends time, a legacy that grows stronger with every interaction, every conversation, every gesture of kindness and understanding. Your customers won't just return for the products or services you offer—they'll return because they believe in you, because they know that you care about them as people, not just as sources of revenue.

This is the kind of relationship-driven success that Clara built. It wasn't a fleeting success built on trends or gimmicks—it was a lasting legacy built on authenticity, trust, and a deep commitment to creating meaningful connections. It's a reminder that in business, as in life, the true measure of success isn't about what you sell or how much you sell it for. It's about the relationships you build, the trust you earn, and the difference you makein the lives of those you serve.

So, how can you ensure that your customers will stay with you forever? The answer is simple, though profound: create an experience that speaks to the heart. Build relationships that go beyond the transaction, that evolve with your customers, and that show them, time and again, that they matter. When you do this, you don't just gain loyal customers—you gain lifelong advocates who will stand by you, year after year, no matter what challenges the future holds. This is how you create not just a business, but a legacy—a legacy of trust, connection, and lasting relationships that will continue to thrive, long into the future.

CHAPTER 19: CONSISTENCY AND STABILITY IN SALES

There's a unique kind of elegance that exists in the mundane—the simple, repeatable actions that others might overlook, but that, when done consistently, yield extraordinary results. In the world of sales, where every transaction can feel like a high-stakes negotiation, the greatest strength is often the simplest one: consistency. Consistency is not flashy. It is not about the one-off big win or the monumental breakthrough. It is about showing up, day in and day out, with a commitment to delivering the same level of excellence. It is the quiet, behind-the-scenes force that builds trust, fosters loyalty, and sets the foundation for long-term success.

Sale isn't a sprint. It's not about racing to close deals, hustling through numbers, or rushing to the next opportunity. Rather, sales is a marathon. It's about steady, intentional progress, one step at a time. And in this marathon, consistency and stability are the keys that unlock lasting relationships with customers, sustained growth, and a reputation that stands the test of time. These traits are the difference between being a company that gets lucky with a few great deals and one that builds an empire of trust, respect, and reliability.

LESSONS FROM THE EVERYDAY

One of the most powerful lessons I've learned in my sales career came from an unlikely source: a local coffee shop. It wasn't a grand, upscale café with fancy machines or exclusive blends, nor was it the kind of place that boasted cutting-edge trends. It was simply a small, neighborhood spot known for its unremarkable décor and basic coffee menu. Yet, the line outside the door every morning was longer than most high-end establishments. Why? It wasn't because the coffee was the best in town—though it was good. It was because the experience, day after day, was predictable, reliable, and exactly what every customer needed.

You see, the owner, a woman named Caroline, wasn't trying to reinvent the wheel. She wasn't offering gourmet coffee or exotic brews that could only be found on Instagram. No, she offered something much more valuable: consistency. Every morning, you could walk into that shop and expect to see Caroline behind the counter, greeting each customer by name. You could expect the same warm smile, the same "How's your day going?" and the same perfectly brewed cup of coffee. And it wasn't just the coffee—it was the entire experience. The same staff, the same routine, the same attention to detail.

At first glance, it didn't seem like much. But it didn't take long before I realized that the real magic of the shop wasn't in the coffee—it was in the stability and predictability of the experience. When you walked into Caroline's shop, you knew exactly what you were going to get. The consistency became so ingrained that it became part of the ritual for many customers. You'd see people come in every morning, get their cup of coffee, chat with Caroline for a moment, and walk out with a smile. It was simple, it was familiar, and it was exactly what they wanted.

In the same way, customers in the world of sales want to know what they're getting. They want the experience to be stable, predictable, and dependable. Whether it's the quality of the product, the service, or the support, your customers want to know that when they engage with your brand, they're going to get exactly what they expect, every time.

THE CYCLE OF TRUST

Consistency doesn't just create a positive customer experience. It builds something much deeper: trust. Trust is the foundation upon which all successful sales are built, and it's not something that can be gained in asingle moment. Trust takes time. It takes repeated interactions. It's formed over many small, seemingly insignificant moments that add up to a larger, more meaningful relationship.

Think about it: When you've experienced the same level of service, quality, and reliability time and time again, you begin to trust that the next experience will be just as good—or better. If a customer buys a product from you and the experience is flawless, they're more likely to return. But if they buy that same product again and find that it doesn't meet the same standard, the trust that was once established begins to erode.

Here's where the power of consistency really comes into play. Every time you interact with a customer, you're reinforcing that trust—or undermining it. Let's say a customer buys a product from you, and it works just as promised. That's great, but that's only one small step in the journey. If you follow up with them consistently—checking in to see how the product is performing, asking if they need any assistance, providing updates when relevant—you are deepening the relationship. You are showing them that you care, that you are reliable, and that they can trust you to deliver, not just once, but over and over again.

I remember working with a client years ago who had purchased a high-endproduct from our company. It wasn't cheap, and it wasn't something that most people would consider an impulse buy. But the customer trusted us. Why? Because we had built a relationship based on consistency. We didn't just send them a brochure and wait for them to decide. We provided constant updates, checked in periodically, and ensured they had all the information they needed to make an informed decision. And, most importantly, we delivered on every promise we made.

When the time came for the customer to make another purchase, they didn't hesitate. They knew we were dependable. They knew we would be there to support them, not just in the beginning but throughout their entire journey with us. They trusted us because, over time, we had shown that we could consistently meet their expectations.

This is the power of trust built on consistency. It's a cycle. The more consistently you deliver, the more trust you build. And the more trust you build, the more likely your customers are to return, recommend your products, and stay loyal to your brand.

THE DANGER OF INCONSISTENCY

As much as consistency can strengthen your sales efforts, inconsistency can have the opposite effect. The damage caused by inconsistency is not always immediately apparent, but it is always significant. Unlike the occasional stumble, which can often be forgiven, inconsistency sends a much more harmful message: that you are unreliable, that you cannot be counted on, and that your brand does not follow through.

I once worked with a company that had a stellar product, but their customerservice was anything but stellar. On one occasion, a customer reached out with an issue regarding a defective product. The customer support team was quick to respond, offered an immediate resolution, and sent the replacement with an apology and a discount for future purchases. Everything seemed fine, and the customer was satisfied.

But then something strange happened. On another occasion, another customer reached out with a similar issue, only to be met with long wait times, conflicting information from different representatives, and no follow-up at all. The customer felt neglected and, eventually, they left the brand for good.

Why? Inconsistency. The first customer was impressed by the prompt, caring response. The second customer, however, felt abandoned by the lack of follow-through and the broken promise of timely service.

It's easy to think that one instance of poor service won't affect your reputation, but in reality, these small inconsistencies can snowball. Word of mouth travels fast, especially in today's connected world. If customers start to feel like they cannot rely on you, they won't hesitate to take theirbusiness elsewhere—and they'll make sure their network knows why.

Consistency is not just about keeping promises; it's about reinforcing those promises at every touchpoint. Whether it's a phone call, an email, or a face-to-face interaction, you must provide a consistent experience that reinforces the trust you've built with your customers.

SYSTEMS, PROCESSES, AND PEOPLE

In order to create a truly consistent sales experience, you need more than just a commitment to delivering excellent service. You need systems and processes in place to ensure that every interaction, every sale, and every customer journey is as predictable as possible. Without these, you leave room for human error, miscommunication, and inconsistency.

This is where stability comes in. Stability in sales doesn't just come from the quality of your product or the friendliness of your team. It comes from creating a structure that allows for dependable outcomes, no matter who is in charge. You need a clearly defined sales process, a set of best practices, and a culture of accountability. When your sales process is stable, your team knows exactly what to expect, and so do your customers.

Take, for example, a company I worked with that implemented a customerrelationship management (CRM) system. Before the CRM, the sales team was all over the place—missed follow-ups, forgotten details, lost opportunities. After the CRM was implemented, everything changed. Every lead was tracked. Every communication was logged. Every promise was documented. No customer was ever forgotten. No opportunity was ever lost.

It wasn't the system itself that made the difference. It was the consistency it allowed. The stability of knowing that every lead would be followed up on time, every communication would be noted, and every customer would receive the attention they deserved.

THE LONG-TERM BENEFITS OF CONSISTENCY

You may find yourself asking, "Is it really worth it?" Is the effort, the dedication, the relentless pursuit of consistency truly going to pay off in the end? The simple, straightforward answer is a resounding yes. While it may seem like the journey towards success is slow and painstaking, thetruth is that the long-term benefits far, far outweigh the immediate grind. In fact, when you step back and look at the bigger picture, the power of consistency becomes abundantly clear—it's not just an investment in today, but in tomorrow and beyond.

In the beginning, it might feel like a slow burn, with every action you take, every step forward, seeming to lack the immediate payoff you might be hoping for. You may feel like you're treading water, putting in the hours, making decisions, and yet, the rewards aren't as instant or as visible as you'd like them to be. But here's where the magic lies: over time, consistency builds momentum. It's like a snowball rolling down a hill. At first, it's small, unassuming, almost insignificant. But with every passing day, with every consistent action, it begins to grow. It compiles. It accumulates.

As you stay the course, doing the work, showing up, and being reliable in what you offer, you create an environment where your customers—your audience—begin to understand exactly what they can expect from you. They learn your rhythm, your reliability, your consistency, and they come to count on it. This level of predictability is invaluable. It isn't just a nice-to-have; it's the foundation of trust. And that trust is everything in the marketplace. Over time, that trust becomes so deeply ingrained in your customers' minds that it forms the bedrock of a loyal, ever-growing customer base.

But here's where it gets even more powerful: consistency isn't just about showing up day after day, week after week. It's about creating a legacy. When you are consistent, when you stand by your promises, when you deliver on what you say you will, you aren't merely succeeding in the moment. You are laying the groundwork for something much larger. You're creating a brand—a reputation—that doesn't just serve you today, but also paves the way for tomorrow's opportunities. It's about building something enduring, something that endures the tests of time, challenges, and shifting market dynamics. You're not just seeking fleeting wins; you're building a lasting legacy that will stand the test of time.

This kind of consistency creates a brand that isn't just well-known, but also well-loved. Your customers will trust you. They will respect you. And they will keep coming back. Because when consistency becomes the hallmark of your brand, it fosters a deep, unwavering connection with your audience. It's no longer about just making a sale—it's about building a relationship. A relationship that goes beyond transactional exchanges and into the realm of trust, loyalty, and genuine respect. It's about creating an emotional bond that keeps customers returning not just because they need your product or service, but because they believe in what you do, in how you do it, and in the promise you've made to them.

And this stability, this foundation of trust and loyalty, is priceless. It is the kind of stability that will weather every storm, face every challenge, and persist even when the market shifts. Stability isn't just a competitive advantage—it's the very thing that will set you apart in a world that is constantly changing, a world where trends come and go, and where the next big thing is always on the horizon. When you have built trust, backed by the consistency of your actions and the integrity of your brand, you create something that stands firm, no matter what comes next.

In the grand scheme of things, sales isn't just about making one-off deals. It's not about closing a single transaction and moving on to the next. It's about fostering relationships—long-term, meaningful relationships. Relationships that are built on trust, reinforced by consistency, and solidified by stability. That's the foundation of long-term success. That's the principle that will always be relevant, no matter what changes in the market, in technology, or in consumer behavior. Consistency will never go out of style. It will always be the silent force that propels your business forward, creating not just success, but significance.

So, if you're wondering whether all this effort, all this dedication to consistency, is truly worth it, remember this: it's not just about what you're achieving today—it's about the future you're building. It's about cultivating trust, creating relationships, and building a legacy that will sustain and elevate your brand for years to come. The short-term hustle may feel taxing, but the long-term rewards are invaluable. And those rewards? They'll be the very thing that allows your business to thrive, longafter the competition has fallen away.

CHAPTER 20: CONCLUSION AND APPLICATION

As we approach the final chapter of this transformative journey, I invite you to pause for a moment of reflection. What we've ventured through together in the pages of this book has been much more than a simple exploration of customer service theories, concepts, and strategies. It has been a profound exploration into the very heart of what makes a business not only successful but truly great. At the core of every thriving organization lies the ability to deeply connect with its customers, creating relationships that are meaningful, lasting, and impactful. And it's not just about meeting expectations; it's about exceeding them, delighting customers in ways that surprise and inspire loyalty.

Throughout our time together, you've absorbed wisdom from some of the world's most successful companies and their customer service practices. You've learned from their triumphs, their failures, and the lessons that shaped them into the exceptional brands they are today. These companies didn't merely survive in a competitive marketplace—they flourished, often disrupting industries, reimagining customer experiences, and, in many cases, setting new benchmarks for excellence. They didn't just meet the standards—they raised them to new heights. And in doing so, they transformed the very landscape of customer expectations, making it more challenging for businesses to simply 'get by.' These businesses didn't just aim to please their customers—they strived to build lifelong relationships, to forge deep connections that would stand the test of time.

But now, the most pressing question you must ask yourself is: How will you apply these principles in your own world? How will you take the knowledge you've gained in this book—knowledge that has been honed and tested through years of real-world application—and breathe life into it within your own business? It's one thing to understand the strategies thatsuccessful businesses have used; it's an entirely different challenge to implement them in your own day-to-day operations. The task at hand is not to simply learn about customer service, but to immerse yourself in these principles, to integrate them into the very fabric of your business, and to make them a natural part of every interaction, every process, every decision.

As you stand on the precipice of this final chapter, I want to encourage you to look at the knowledge and insights you've gained not as a collection of abstract ideas, but as a powerful toolkit. This toolkit, when used correctly, has the potential to reshape your business in profound ways. Butthe question remains: How will you translate these principles into action? How will you shift from understanding to doing, from theory to practice?

By the end of this chapter, my goal is not just to provide a summary of everything we've discussed, but to ensure that you are fully equipped totake the first crucial steps toward building a legacy of customer service excellence that will endure long into the future. A legacy built on more than just transactional exchanges but on deep, meaningful relationships with the people who matter most: your customers. A legacy where every touchpoint, every interaction, every moment spent with a customer reinforces their trust in your brand and strengthens the bond between you. This legacy will not be built overnight, nor will it be easy. But with patience, commitment, and a relentless focus on your customers, it is not only achievable—it is inevitable.

So, as we bring this chapter to a close, I urge you to take a deep breath. Take a moment to reflect on everything you've absorbed. Now, let's begin to take all the pieces we've explored, all the concepts and strategies, and weave them together into a comprehensive, actionable plan. A plan that will guide you as you step forward into the future with a renewed sense of purpose and determination. A plan that will set you on a path toward not just achieving success but creating a lasting impact that will resonate with your customers and elevate your business for years to come.

It's time to stop thinking about what could be and start acting on what will be. The time for change is now. The opportunity to build a customer service legacy that will not only elevate your brand but also redefine the standards of excellence in your industry is right in front of you. You have everything you need to succeed, and now it's time to take that first step toward transforming your business into a customer service powerhouse.

Let's get started.

THE ROAD TO IMPLEMENTATION: ONE STEP AT A TIME

Picture this: you've just opened a small café in a vibrant, bustling part of the city. The kind of place where the smells of freshly brewed coffee and warm pastries beckon to passersby. Your vision is clear and ambitious: you're not just selling coffee; you're selling an experience. A warm, inviting place where people can come not only for their morning caffeine fix but to escape the busyness of life, connect with others, and leave feelingbetter than when they arrived.

At the core of this vision lies one central idea: exceptional customer service is the key to success. It's the bridge between just another ordinary business and a beloved establishment that people talk about, recommend to friends, and return to again and again. And it's not just about providing good service; it's about going above and beyond—creating experiences, building relationships, and making your customers feel truly special.

But how do you turn that vision into a reality? How do you take the ideals you've learned about and transform them into daily actions that will make your business stand out from the crowd? The answer is simpler than you might think. It starts with a commitment to small, consistent steps, rooted in one overarching philosophy: customer service is not just a department or a set of procedures; it's the heart and soul of your entire business.

STEP 1: CULTIVATE A HEART OF SERVICE

Before you can ever expect your customers to feel valued, you must first create a culture where service is revered and celebrated. It starts with you, the leader of your business. Your attitude, your mindset, and the values you hold will directly impact the way your team approaches customer service. And this, in turn, will influence the way your customers feel whenthey interact with your business.

Take a moment and think about the businesses that you've personally interacted with that made a lasting impression on you. What was it about their service that made it stand out? Perhaps it was the genuine smile of the employee, or the way they remembered your name after just one visit. Maybe it was the extra mile they went to make sure you were satisfied, even when things didn't go according to plan. Whatever it was, these businesses created a sense of belonging and care that left you feeling more than just like a customer—they made you feel like you mattered.

Now, imagine you're the owner of this café. You have the opportunity, every day, to create these kinds of moments for your customers. And it starts with your attitude. If you genuinely care about your customers—if you make it your mission to serve them with kindness, patience, and respect—your team will follow suit. Service is not just a skill; it's a mindset, a philosophy, and a way of life.

You could start by sitting down with your team and sharing with them the heart of your business: the importance of treating each customer like they are the most important person in the room. Share stories of exceptional service, not as a means of instruction, but as a source of inspiration. Explain that their job is not just to serve coffee; their job is to serve people—people who are walking in with unique needs, hopes, and stories.

"Our goal is simple," you might say to your team, "We're here to make someone's day better. Every day. We're not just serving coffee. We're serving experiences, memories, and connections. When we do that, we'll not only build a loyal customer base, but we'll create an atmosphere where people feel valued, respected, and at home."

By framing service in this way, you're not just teaching your team to perform a task; you're inviting them to be part of something larger. You're giving them a sense of purpose and ownership over the customer experience.

STEP 2: KNOW YOUR CUSTOMERS BY NAME, AND THEIR NEEDS BY HEART

As the café grows and more people begin to walk through the doors, it becomes clear that knowing your customers on a personal level is one of the most powerful tools in creating loyalty. There's an old saying: "People don't care how much you know until they know how much you care." And that's exactly what your customers are looking for. They don't want to feel like just another transaction in your day—they want to feel like individuals who matter.

The first step in achieving this is to learn their names. It may seem like a small detail, but it's one of the most powerful ways to make someone feel important. Imagine Sarah, the young professional who walks in every morning for her usual caramel macchiato. The next time she comes in, you greet her with a warm smile and say, "Good morning, Sarah! The usual today?"

It might seem like a small gesture, but it makes a world of difference. Now, Sarah feels recognized. She feels like she's not just a stranger in a sea of customers—she's a person who is seen and valued. And the beauty of it is that it doesn't just stop with Sarah. Every customer who walks in gets the same treatment. Whether they're a regular or a first-timer, you make it a point to remember their names, their preferences, and their unique personalities.

But it's not just about names. As you get to know your customers, you begin to understand their deeper needs. Perhaps Sarah is a bit shy and tends to sit quietly in the corner, reading her book while sipping her coffee. One day, you notice that she seems a bit down, and without saying anything, you take her usual order and bring it to her with a small note that says, "We hope your day gets better. You're awesome."

This personal touch may be small, but it speaks volumes. It shows Sarah that you're not just interested in her business— you care about her well- being. That emotional connection is what will turn a one-time customer into a lifelong advocate for your café. It's about making your customers feel like they belong, like they're part of something bigger than just a transaction.

STEP 3: CONSISTENCY IS THE HEARTBEAT OF YOUR BUSINESS

As your business grows, the challenge becomes not just about creating great service in the moment, but about ensuring that the experience is consistent, day in and day out. You can't afford to have days where the service is exceptional and other days where it falls short. Consistency is what builds trust, and trust is what keeps customers coming back.

How do you ensure that every customer, no matter when they walk in, gets the same level of service? It starts with systems. Systems are the backbone of any successful business. They ensure that no matter who is behind the counter or what the circumstances are, the service you provide will always be top-notch.

You might implement a system for tracking customer preferences, making sure that each team member is aware of the small details that matter. Perhaps you create a checklist for every customer interaction, ensuring that the little things—like greeting the customer with a smile, taking their order promptly, and thanking them for their business—never get overlooked.

But systems aren't just about efficiency; they're about maintaining quality. They ensure that no matter how busy the day gets, every customer is treated with the same level of care and respect. Consistency doesn't mean being robotic; it means delivering a service experience that is predictable, reliable, and memorable every single time.

STEP 4: BUILD LOYALTY THROUGH EMOTIONAL CONNECTIONS

Once you've mastered the art of consistency, it's time to take things to the next level: creating emotional connections. Your customers should feel like they're not just coming to your café to get a cup of coffee—they should feel like they're coming home. This is where the magic happens.

Loyalty isn't built on discounts or special offers (though those can help). It's built on emotional connections—connections that make your customers feel like they're part of your family. You can create these connections by celebrating milestones with your customers, like birthdays, anniversaries, or even the small victories of their everyday lives. Maybe you remember that Sarah loves a particular pastry, and one day, you surprise her with it, just because.

Or perhaps you create a rewards program where customers get special perks for being loyal. But don't just make the rewards about getting free items—make them about creating experiences. For example, you might offer a "VIP experience" where your loyal customers get a special tasting session of new drinks before they're officially released.

Emotional connections are what turn customers into brand advocates. When people feel valued and appreciated, they want to share that experience with others. They'll tell their friends and family about the wonderful café that made them feel like family, and soon enough, your café will be buzzing with new customers who can't wait to experience that same level of care.

STEP 5: GROW THROUGH FEEDBACK

Feedback is the mirror that reflects how well you're doing and where you can improve. It's easy to assume that everything is going great, especially when business is thriving. But the truth is, there are always areas where you can improve. And the best way to find out where those areas are is to ask your customers.

Encourage feedback through surveys, online reviews, or simply by asking your customers how their experience was. And when you receive negative feedback, don't take it personally—take it as an opportunity to learn. Thank your customers for being honest, and make a plan to fix whatever went wrong.

STEP 6: STAY COMMITTED, NO MATTER THE CHALLENGES

Running a business is not for the faint of heart. There will be days when things aren't going according to plan, when customers are difficult, or when the line is longer than you'd like. But the key to success is perseverance. You can't let setbacks or challenges derail your commitment to providing exceptional service.

The road to building a legendary brand is long, but if you

stay true to your vision, your values, and your commitment to your customers, you'll build something that lasts.

A FINAL WORD

As we draw this book to a close, it's important to reflect on the significanceof the journey we've embarked on together. The pursuit of customer service excellence is not something that can be achieved through a single moment of inspiration, nor can it be completed after reading a few pages of advice. It is, in fact, a lifelong commitment—a path that requires continuous learning, adapting, and evolving. Every day offers a new opportunity to make an impactful difference in someone's life, to craft experiences that transcend the moment and linger in the hearts and minds of those you serve long after they've walked out your café doors.

The true essence of exceptional customer service lies in the small, oftenunnoticed gestures. It's in the friendly greeting that welcomes your customers as soon as they step through the door, the attention to detail in the way you serve them, and the care with which you handle any challenges that may arise. Each interaction is a chance to not only satisfy a need but to also delight, inspire, and create a lasting impression. The beauty of customer service is that it goes beyond just delivering a product or service; it's about crafting an experience—an experience that feels personal, unique, and memorable. It's about treating every customer as if they are the most important person in the room, because, in that moment, they are.

As you move forward from this point, understand that the insights, strategies, lessons, and stories we've shared are merely the beginning of your journey toward mastering the art of customer service. These are the tools you will use to build not just a business, but a legacy. A legacy rooted in genuine care, mutual respect, and unwavering commitment to those you serve. The skills you've honed here are meant to be nurtured, practiced, and expanded upon every single day. The key to sustained success lies in your ability to consistently deliver exceptional service, not as a one-time effort, but as an ongoing practice.

This is your invitation to go forth with unshakable confidence, knowing this: By embracing the principles of customer service, you are doing more than simply growing your business—you are cultivating a movement. A movement that will not only enhance the lives of your customers but also inspire others in your community and industry to adopt the same approach. It is through your commitment to excellence that you will set the standard for what great customer service can look like, and in doing so, you'll inspire those around you to follow suit, creating a ripple effect that will resonate for years to come.

By continuously striving to create positive, memorable experiences for your customers, you are contributing to a culture of service that transcends any single transaction. You are fostering relationships, building trust, and reinforcing the idea that exceptional service is not an exception, but the standard. As you continue to refine and apply these strategies, remember that every positive interaction has the potential to inspire change, to build community, and to create a movement that can influence not only the success of your business but also the way others think about and approach customer service in their own lives.

So, as you step into the future, equipped with the knowledge and insights from this book, I encourage you to keep pushing the boundaries of whatexcellent service can look like. Let your actions be a testament to your dedication, your passion, and your commitment to making a difference. The world of customer service is vast and ever-evolving, but one thing is certain: with the right mindset, a heart dedicated to service, and the tools you've gained from this book, you are more than prepared to leave an indelible mark on the world of customer service, creating a lasting legacy of excellence that will inspire generations to come.

REFERENCES

The Bible provides an abundance of wisdom on the way we should approach our work, serve others, and maintain our relationships, particularly in the context of business. The scriptures offer invaluable teachings on how to treat people with respect, kindness, integrity, and fairness—principles that are foundational to successful customer service. When we turn to the Word of God, we find timeless guidance that helps us align our business practices and interpersonal interactions with the character of Christ.

At the heart of excellent customer service lies the commandment of love that Jesus outlines in Matthew 22:37-39. In this passage, Jesus summarizes the essence of all the law and the prophets, stating, "Love the Lord your God with all your heart, with all your soul, and with all your mind. This is the first and greatest commandment. And the second is like it: Love your neighbor as yourself." In these two powerful statements, Jesus calls us to prioritize love above all else, which becomes the foundation for how we interact with others in every area of life, including in business. By loving our neighbors as ourselves, we put their needs, desires, and concerns at the forefront of our actions, ensuring that every encounter is characterized by empathy, compassion, and care. This loving approach is critical in customer service, as it allows us to go beyond simply fulfilling a need, and instead create a positive, life-affirming experience for everyone we serve.

Paul, in Philippians 2:3-4, also echoes the importance of considering others above ourselves, writing, "Do nothing out of selfish ambition or vain conceit. Rather, in humility, value others above yourselves, not looking to your own interests but each of you to the interests of the others." Here, the apostle highlights the virtue of humility, which is essential to customer service. The idea of putting the interests of others above our own is a direct challenge to a culture that often elevates self-interest and individual gain. In customer service, this means that we should be more concerned with the customer's needs than with the profit we stand to make.

It involves listening carefully to their concerns, providing helpful and thoughtful solutions, and giving of ourselves in ways that may not always be immediately profitable but are always valuable in the long term.

The role of honesty and integrity is emphasized throughout the scriptures, and these principles are vital in building trust with customers. Proverbs 12:22 declares, "The Lord detests lying lips, but he delights in people who are trustworthy." Trust is the foundation of all meaningful relationships, and it is the same in business. Customers place their trust in companies to provide them with reliable products, services, and information. If a business fails to be honest or transparent, it risks losing that trust, and the customer may never return. On the other hand, when businesses consistently demonstrate truthfulness, they foster an environment of reliability, where customers feel safe and valued. This commitment to integrity in every interaction helps build a strong reputation, both with individual customers and the broader community.

Moreover, Jesus Christ Himself provides the ultimate example of servant leadership and selfless service. In John 13:12-17, we see Jesus washing the feet of His disciples, an act of extreme humility that would have been considered a lowly task in the cultural context of that time. Jesus, though the Son of God, took on the role of a servant to demonstrate the importance of humility in leadership and service. After washing their feet, He instructed His disciples, saying, "Now that I, your Lord and Teacher, have washed your feet, you also should wash one another's feet." This profound act illustrates that no act of service is too small or too insignificant when done in love. The lesson for us in business is clear: whether we are engaging in high-level strategic decisions or responding to a customer's complaint, every act of service is valuable and worthy of our utmost care and attention.

In the Book of Colossians, Paul further elaborates on the Christian's approach to work. Colossians 3:23-24 provides a powerful principle that should guide anyone in customer service or business: "Whatever you do, work at it with all your heart, as working for the Lord, not for human masters, since you know that you will receive an inheritance from the Lord as a reward. It is the Lord Christ you are serving." This passage teaches that no matter the task, no matter how mundane or routine it may seem, we should approach it with excellence because ultimately, our service is to God. When we adopt this perspective, we elevate every task, no matter how seemingly insignificant, into an act of worship. This mindset compels us to serve our customers with enthusiasm, diligence, and care, knowing that our efforts, though unseen by many, are deeply valued by God.

The wisdom of Proverbs further contributes to our understanding of how to build trust and credibility, which are crucial in any business, especially in customer service. Proverbs 22:1 reminds us, "A good name is more desirable than great riches; to be esteemed is better than silver or gold." Reputation is invaluable, and a strong reputation can be earned through honesty, integrity, and a commitment to quality service. For businesses, maintaining a good reputation is crucial to long-term success, as customersare more likely to return to a company that is trustworthy and known for delivering excellent service. It takes years to build a reputation, but onlymoments to destroy it. Therefore, businesses must continually strive to maintain a high standard of service and character in every interaction.

James 1:19 teaches us about the importance of patience, especially in difficult situations, which is another critical aspect of customer service. "Everyone should be quick to listen, slow to speak and slow to become angry." This advice is especially important when dealing with unhappy or frustrated customers. A calm, patient response can defuse a tense situation and turn a negative experience into a positive one. When we take the time to listen to customers and understand their concerns before responding, wedemonstrate respect for their feelings and ensure that our solutions are tailored to meet their needs. In the fast-paced world of business, patience may sometimes seem in short supply, but it is precisely in these moments that we can make the most profound impact by embodying the love andgentleness of Christ.

Loyalty and commitment to our customers is another significant theme found in the Bible. Proverbs 3:3-4 emphasizes the value of love and faithfulness in relationships, saying, "Let love and faithfulness never leave you; bind them around your neck, write them on the tablet of your heart. Then you will win favor and a good name in the sight of God and man." Loyalty in business translates to consistency and dependability. It means that customers can count on you to deliver on your promises and offer support even after the transaction has been completed. When businesses demonstrate loyalty by maintaining high standards, providing ongoing customer care, and honoring their commitments, they create lasting relationships with customers who will return time and again.

Furthermore, the Bible teaches us that the rewards of good service are not only temporal but eternal. In Matthew 25:21, Jesus speaks to the faithful servant, saying, "Well done, good and faithful servant... come and share your master's happiness." This statement reveals the joy that comes from serving others well, not just in a business context, but in all areas of life. When we serve others with love and integrity, we reflect the character of Christ, and we participate in the fulfillment of His Kingdom work on Earth. The ultimate reward for excellent service is not earthly wealth or accolades but the joy and satisfaction of knowing we have pleased God and fulfilled His will for our lives.

Finally, the Bible continually emphasizes the importance of treating others with respect, dignity, and fairness. Romans 12:10 offers a powerful reminder: "Be devoted to one another in love. Honor one another above yourselves." In customer service, this principle means that we should not view customers merely as individuals we are trying to sell to or serve, but as people worthy of our time, care, and attention. We should honor their needs, provide them with the highest level of service possible, and treat them as we would like to be treated ourselves. This Golden Rule, as found in Matthew 7:12, "So in everything, do to others what you would have them do to you," forms the foundation for treating customers with kindness, respect, and empathy.

The lessons found in the Bible are as relevant today as they have ever been, especially in the context of business and customer service. By embracing the principles of love, humility, integrity, patience, and loyalty, we can create a business environment that not only meets the needs of our customers but also reflects the character of Christ. When we approach our work with these biblical values in mind, we are not merely performing tasks or engaging in transactions; we are living out our faith in tangible ways, showing the world the love, grace, and excellence of God through our service. In this way, customer service becomes more than just a business function—it becomes a ministry, an opportunity to demonstrate God's love in action, and a chance to make a lasting impact on the lives of those we serve.

SOURCES

1. **"The Nordstrom Way To Customer Experience Excellence"** by Robert Spector and BreAnne O. Reeves

- This book offers strategies and practices that can elevate customer service, focusing on personalizing experiences, creatingloyalty, and handling customers with care.

2. **"Delivering Happiness: A Path To Profits, Passion, AndPurpose"** by Tony Hsieh

- A renowned book that discusses how the CEO of Zappos built acustomer-centric company by fostering a culture of serviceexcellence.

3. **"The Effortless Experience: Conquering The New Battleground For Customer Loyalty"** by Matthew Dixon,Nick Toman, and Rick DeLisi

- This book covers key skills like problem-solving, customerloyalty, and how minimizing customer effort leads to satisfaction.

ARTICLES AND RESEARCH PAPERS:

1. **HARVARD BUSINESS REVIEW: "UNDERSTANDINGCUSTOMER SERVICE"**

- A comprehensive resource on customer behavior, satisfaction metrics, and how to design a customer experience strategy.

2. FORBES: "THE FUTURE OF CUSTOMER SERVICE: 20 EXPERT PREDICTIONS"

- Discusses emerging trends in customer service, especially in the digital age, and how companies can keep up with customer expectations.

3. McKinsey & Company: "Customer Experience: Creating Value Through Transformative Customer Journeys"

- This article explains how businesses can build loyalty and long-term success by focusing on understanding customer journeys.

ONLINE RESOURCES:

1. HELP SCOUT BLOG

- A valuable blog with practical insights on building a customer support team, emphasizing skills like communication, empathy, and time management.

2. ZENDESK CUSTOMER EXPERIENCE TRENDS

- Provides insights into customer service trends, the impact of technology on service delivery, and how customer expectations areevolving.

3. SALESFORCE'S "STATE OF THE CONNECTED CUSTOMER" REPORT

- This report shares global insights on customer behavior andexpectations, crucial for any customer service strategy.

PRACTICAL GUIDES:

1. **"Customer Service for Dummies"** by Karen Leland and KeithBailey

- A user-friendly guide that breaks down basic and advancedcustomer service skills.
2. "The Customer Rules: The 39 Essential Rules for DeliveringSensational Service" by Lee Cockerell

A practical guidebook that highlights the do's and don'ts of customer service, useful for building effective customer interactions.

CUSTOMER SERVICE SKILLS